BRADFORD CITY
Miscellany

BRADFORD CITY
Miscellany

*Bantams Trivia,
History, Facts & Stats*

DAVID MARKHAM

BRADFORD CITY
Miscellany

Published By:
Pitch Publishing (Brighton) Ltd
A2 Yeoman Gate
Yeoman Way
Durrington
BN13 3QZ

Email: info@pitchpublishing.co.uk
Web: www.pitchpublishing.co.uk

First published 2010
Updated and reprinted 2014, 2017

A catalogue record for this book is available from the British Library.

13-digit ISBN: 978-1-9054117-4-0

Printed and bound in India by Replika Press Pvt. Ltd.

FOREWORD BY TERRY DOLAN

When people ask what is your club I feel well within my rights to say that it's Bradford City. You could class my career as a mirror image of Bradford City in recent years – up and down.

It goes back to being born in Bradford and supporting the club from being six or seven years old. I always wanted to be a professional footballer and to sign as a schoolboy at Valley Parade was a dream come true. Then the manager, Jimmy Wheeler, told me I wasn't good enough.

However, I wasn't going to accept that and I went on to make my league debut for Bradford Park Avenue, which in those days was the enemy as far as I was concerned. Then I had the chance to go to Arsenal but turned it down and went to Huddersfield Town, which was another high because they were in the top division, but they went down to the Fourth Division in the space of five years.

I then returned to Bradford City – the club that had rejected me as a schoolboy. We gained promotion from the Fourth Division in my first season – 1976/77 – only to be relegated the following season. I left Valley Parade to go to Rochdale and when I finished playing I had the opportunity to work for Bradford Council coaching football.

Then I was fortunate that the City manager Trevor Cherry asked me to go back to the club as youth-team coach. I then became assistant manager, and then manager. I was only 37. As manager, I went close to leading the club to the top division – we were beaten in the play-offs. I was so disappointed it didn't happen, we were just a whisper away from doing it, but we had two exciting seasons.

I later managed Rochdale, Hull City and York City and I now work for the League Managers' Association and do referees' assessments for the Premier League, but I still feel a lot for Bradford City and I would like to get involved with them in some capacity, although not as manager.

Enjoy the read

Terry Dolan
Payer 1976–81
Manager 1987–89

ACKNOWLEDGEMENTS

In writing this book, I would like to acknowledge the help I have received from Terry Frost's book, *Bradford City: A Complete Record* published by Breedon in 1988, the files of my old newspaper, the *Bradford Telegraph & Argus* and acknowledge the help given by the staff of Bradford Central Library in perusing their files on microfilm in their archives section.

I have also consulted *The Bradford City Story: The Pain and the Glory*, written by Lindsay Sutton and I, and published by Breedon in 2006, and my own book, *The Legends of Bradford City*, also published by Breedon in 2007. I consulted at length *Bantams over Wembley: Bradford City's Miracle Season* by Gary Jones and Dave Fletcher. I am also grateful to the Spartacus Educational website for information about Fatty Foulke and the book *A Game that Would Play* by A J Arnold. I am also indebted to my daughter-in-law, Janette Markham, whose computer skills have helped me enormously in the editing and transmission process.

I would also like to thank Pitch Publishing for giving me the opportunity to write the book and for their help and guidance in the production process. Finally, I thank my wife Susan for her patience and encouragement in this project.

INTRODUCTION

In writing *Miscellany*, I have tried to capture some of the highs and lows of Bradford City's 110-year history and the personalities that shaped these events on and off the field.

From the highs of winning the FA Cup in 1911, a mere eight years after they were formed, to the lows of seeking re-election to the old Fourth Division, all these events are recorded here.

All clubs have their ups and downs during their history and, while City have won championships and played in the Premier League, they have also suffered more financial crises than most clubs, as well as the 1985 fire disaster, when 56 people lost their lives. These and other events are analysed in *Bradford City Miscellany*.

The book also charts the somewhat unusual beginnings of Bradford City. The oldest club in West Yorkshire, they were admitted to the Football League in 1903 without playing a competitive match because the football authorities wanted to gain a foothold in what was regarded as a rugby stronghold.

City used to be Manningham Rugby Club, but the rugby committee decided to switch to soccer because it was a game 'that would pay.' So, the club became part of the fast growing sport of football. This is a celebration of the vision of the founding fathers that made that momentous decision. However, none of the founders of Bradford City could have imagined the phenomenal growth of football, the global game, played in all corners of the world and enjoyed in every country through the medium of television and the internet.

Back in Bradford, having suffered three relegations in six years – in 2002, 2004 and 2007 – City began back the long climb back following an extraordinary season in 2012-13, in which the club appeared twice in a Wembley final, beating three Premier League clubs to reach the League Cup final before returning to Wembley three months later to win the League Two play-final and promotion to League One.

David Markham

IN THE BEGINNING...

The West Riding of Yorkshire was slow to embrace association football, which was expanding rapidly in many other parts of the country in the late Victorian era. However, in 1894, the West Yorkshire League was formed to bring about organised football after local teams had spring up in different parts of the county. Several teams were formed in the Bradford area, among them Buckstone Park, who played at City's current training ground, Apperley Bridge, in the early 1890s before re-naming themselves Bradford FC and moving to Park Avenue. They played their first home match there against Manchester Moss Side in September 1896. So, football was played at Park Avenue before it was staged at Valley Parade! Among its early players were Colonel Armitage, one of the founders of Bradford City, and David Menzies, a player, and later manager, in the 1920s.

RUGBY

Bradford City was born out of a rugby club. Manningham Rugby Football Club were formed in 1880 although the club had been in existence for at least four years as Manningham Albion and in 1886 they moved to Valley Parade from Carlisle Road, about half a mile away. In 1895 Manningham were one of the founder members of a new rugby code, Rugby league, formed after disagreement over broken time payments to players, and they won the championship in the first season of the competition.

Interestingly, their rugby competitors across the city were Bradford Rugby Football Club, who later became Bradford (Park Avenue) AFC and, when they too switched to soccer, the City-Avenue rivalry was born. Manningham decided to switch to association football during the 1902/03 rugby season because they were in financial difficulties and they thought soccer would a better commercial proposition – in their words "a game that would pay". How right they were. And so, after a 75-34 vote in favour of a switch of codes at the club's annual meeting, the committee formed a football club and applied for membership of the Football League. So keen were the league – formed 15 years earlier in 1988 – to gain a foothold in West Yorkshire, then considered to be a rugby stronghold, that they elected City to the Football League on May 25th, 1903, replacing Doncaster Rovers in the Second Division, even though they had never played a competitive match.

The man who put forward the idea that Bradford could support a Football League club was a journalist called James Whyte. The sub editor on the Bradford Observer had played soccer in his native Scotland and, after many set backs, he attended a private meeting of Manningham Football Club at Valley Parade at the end of January 1903. The meeting led to a series of other meetings before the rugby club agreed to pursue the idea of switching from rugby league to professional football and try to gain election to the Football League. To stimulate interest in football in Bradford, a promotional match was arranged between FA Cup winners Sheffield United, and a team of local amateurs.

Then, on May 1st, before there was any assurance that the new club would be elected to the Football League, they signed their first two players; centre-half Jack Forrest and inside-right Ben Prosser, both from Stoke City. Sam Bright from Sheffield United, future captain George Robinson from Nottingham Forest, future manager Peter O'Rourke from Chesterfield, and half-back James Millar from Middlesbrough followed soon afterwards. In all, the club spent £917 in putting their squad together. Unusually, City's first captain was chosen by a ballot of players. Following their election to the Football League, the team was hastily recruited by manager Robert Campbell and, as many of the players were not that well known to the directors, it was left to the players to choose their captain. Their choice was insideforward Johnny McMillan, who had joined them from Small Heath – later to become Birmingham City. He had also played for Derby County and Leicester Fosse and, after leaving City in 1906, he signed for Glossop North End before managing Gillingham.

The McMillan family connection with City continued when his son Stuart McMillan, an outside-right, joined them from Wolves in May 1924 and stayed for three years before signing for Nottingham Forest. The new club chose the Manningham Rugby Club's claret and amber as their colours for the newly formed football club. Manningham, formed in 1880, originally played in black shirts and white shorts before settling for claret and amber in September 1884. The colours may have been linked to nearby Belle Vue Barracks, or to the Australian view that claret and amber represented blood and mustard, the fighting qualities of blood and strength. Whatever the origin, the football club decided to play in claret and amber stripes to distinguish them from the rugby club, who played in hoops. After high expectations, City made a disappointing start when they lost their first match 2-0 against Grimsby Town at Valley Parade on the historic day, September 1st, 1903 in front of an estimated crowd of 10,000 – double their expectations.

The new team also lost their second match 3-1 – at Gainsborough Trinity – four days later, but at least they scored and the distinction of scoring the first goal went to outside-right Richard Guy, signed from Manchester City. According to the Daily Argus, the goal was greeted with 'a shout, which awoke the babies on the distant hillsides of Bolton and Eccleshill'. It proved to be the only goal of Guy's brief career with the Bantams, as the player made only nine league and FA Cup appearances before he was transferred to Leeds City at the end of the season.

FIRST VICTORY

City's historic first win came in their third match, 2-0 on a Tuesday evening at Burton United – no connection with the present club Burton Albion. Goalscorers were Jack Forrest and Stuart McMillan and City followed up that victory by beating Bristol City 1-0 at home the following Saturday. McMillan scored the vital goal to the delight of the 16,000 crowd. The size of the crowd proved that football in Bradford had a bright future and vindicated the decision by the Manningham Football Club to switch to soccer. There were ups and downs during City's first season but the club quickly established themselves, finishing in tenth place, while gate receipts amounted to £3,896.

LIMITED

After changing managers in mid-season – Peter O'Rourke replaced their first manager Robert Campbell – City finished the 1905/06 campaign in 11th place, losing a not inconsiderable £320 which made their accumulated deficit £1,074. Dissatisfaction was expressed at the annual meeting in May 1906. A commission of inquiry was set up to investigate the club's accounts and they criticised the way the club was being run. Following their recommendations, it was decided to form a limited company and, although some members opposed this move, fearing they would lose control of the club, a limited company was set up two years later – Bradford City (1908) Ltd.

I NAME THIS FOOTBALL CLUB, BRADFORD CITY...

The formation of a limited company saw a welcome influx of cash through share capital. Although the club had played under the name of Bradford City, they were still incorporated under the Companies Act as Manningham Football Club.

FIRST DIVISION BECKONS

The injection of share capital was used to fund ground improvements to make Valley Parade worthy of the First Division following their promotion as Second Division champions in 1908. New stands were erected on the Midland Road and the South Parade – main stand – sides of the ground to provide spectators with cover.

A MERGER?

City had been in existence for only three years when it was proposed that they merge with Bradford Rugby Club, who played at Park Avenue. Bradford RFC couldn't make ends meet playing rugby league and wanted to share in City's early success following their switch from rugby league to association football. City's lease for Valley Parade with the Midland Railway Company had to be renewed every three months with no apparent prospect of a long-term deal.

ALMOST A THOUSAND YEARS ACROSS THE CITY

The club committee also thought that the Valley Parade ground was unfit for First Division crowds should City gain promotion to the top division. Across the city at Park Avenue where Bradford RFC shared facilities with Bradford Cricket Club and Yorkshire County Cricket Club, there was a 999-year lease on the ground.

HISTORICAL DECISION

Given that Park Avenue wanted to give up rugby it was surely logical for the clubs to pool their resources with City moving to Park Avenue, which was in a more pleasant part of the city than inner city Valley Parade with its mills and rows of terraced houses. However, at a meeting of Bradford City members the voting was 1,031 against a merger and 487 for. So, the idea died a death, Bradford Rugby Club became Bradford (Park Avenue) AFC and the rugby people separated to form Bradford Northern.

FATTY

City signed one of the greatest and most outrageous characters in English football when goalkeeper William 'Fatty' Foulke joined them from Chelsea towards the end of the 1905/06 season. Born in 1874, Foulke was renowned for his size – 6ft 4ins tall and reported 24 stone in weight at the end of his career.

He played four first-class cricket matches for Derbyshire, but, of course, he is best known as a footballer. After being discovered playing for his Derbyshire village side at Blackwell, Foulke made his debut for First Division Sheffield United against West Bromwich Albion in September 1894 and led the team to three FA Cup finals and a league championship triumph. It was a golden era for United, who won the cup in 1899 and 1902 and were beaten finalists in 1901. They won the league championship in 1898 and were runners-up in 1897 and 1900. The stories about 'Fatty' Foulke are legendary. At the end of the 1902 FA Cup Final, Foulke protested to the referee that Southampton's equaliser should not have been allowed. So, he left the dressing room naked and pursued the referee, Tom Kirkham, who took refuge in a broom cupboard. So angry was Foulke that a group of FA officials had to stop him from wrenching the cupboard from its hinges to reach the referee. Foulke made several key saves as Sheffield United won the replay 2-1. It is also reported that he brought a Sheffield and Derbyshire League match to a halt by swinging on a crossbar and breaking it.

He moved to Chelsea – then, like City, a Second Division club – for a fee of £50 and was made club captain, but by then his behaviour was becoming even more eccentric. If he thought his defenders were not trying hard enough he would leave the field. Opposing forwards who displeased him would be picked up and thrown into his goal. Not surprisingly, Foulke became a big crowd puller and Chelsea were keen to exploit his boxoffice potential. To draw attention to his size, the club placed two small boys behind his goal in an effort to distract the opposition. The boys would sometimes return the ball when it went out of play and so, quite by accident, balls boys came into being. After one season at Chelsea, Foulke joined City, signed by the then new manager Peter O'Rourke towards the end of their third season as a league club.

Foulke made his debut in the last match of the season, a 0-0 home draw against Barnsley and was a regular in the first half of the following campaign before retiring when only 32. It is inconceivable that a player so overweight would be a regular player in league football nowadays, but remarkably Foulke made 411 career appearances in all competitions, 24 of them with City, and was a regular in the top division with Sheffield United for 11 seasons between 1894 and 1905. After his football career was over, Foulke, who appears in the Mitchell and Kenyon films playing in a match in September 1902, became an entertainer at Blackpool and earned some money as a 'beat the goalie' booth on the beach.

TITLE TRIUMPHS

City have won three championships in their 107-year history. The first was in 1907/08, only five years after they were formed, when they won the Second Division title – there were only two divisions in those days. They made the best possible start, thrashing Chesterfield 8-1 at home with Wally Smith scoring four goals, and they went on to consolidate that great start by winning five of their first seven matches, including a 5-0 home win over Leeds City. There were few blips that season as City lost only eight of their 38 matches.

They enjoyed a four-match winning run just before the halfway mark of the campaign, a five-match winning sequence just after the halfway mark, and ended the season in style by winning their last five matches. Scottish centre forward Frank O'Rourke, signed just before the end of the previous season from Airdrieonians, proved to be an instant success by top-scoring with 21 goals in 36 league matches, four of them in a 7-1 home win over Gainsborough Trinity. O'Rourke was closely followed by Smith, who scored 20 in 34 league matches while George Handley with 16, and Jimmy McDonald with 13, also reached a double figure number of goals. The second title triumph will be remembered for the number

City scored as the Bantams won the Third Division (North) ...nship with 128 goals – a record for a 42-match programme – but ...rly didn't start the season at all. The club were threatened with ...tion after the players dispersed from the previous campaign with no commitment about their future.

However, thanks to donations from directors and supporters the club survived their financial crisis and the new board of directors produced a masterstroke by bringing the club's most successful manager, Peter O'Rourke, to Valley Parade. O'Rourke had led City to the Second Division championship in 1908, and the FA Cup triumph three years later, and kept them in the First Division before he left a year before they were relegated. In the meantime, he had had a brief spell in Wales as manager of Pontypridd and Dundee Hibernians before returning to Bradford to manage Park Avenue for ten months. The chance to return to Valley Parade tempted him out of retirement and he made an immediate impact – and what an impact. In fact, no-one could have imagined such a spectacular start to the new campaign – a club-record 11-1 thrashing of Rotherham United at Valley Parade – the only time the club have reached double figures in a league match. Trevor Edmunds and Cornelius White, a close-season signing from Bangor, scored hat-tricks, Aubrey Scriven and Edmund Harvey both scored twice and Ralph Burkinshaw scored the other goal.

Not surprisingly, that win was City's biggest of the season, but the 11-goal romp set the tone for a season that 'rained' goals. Other eye-catching scorelines were two consecutive 8-0 home wins in March – against Tranmere Rovers on the Wednesday and Barrow on the Saturday. And, for good measure, City followed up those two emphatic victories with two consecutive 5-0 wins against Chesterfield away, and Wrexham at home. Not only did City have a free-scoring attack, but easily the meanest defence in Division Three (North) that season, conceding only 43 goals. In fact, during a run of five matches in March the team scored 29 goals without reply while, in a 14-match spell, City scored 49 goals while conceding only four. One of manager O'Rourke's masterstrokes was the signing in the February of centre forward Albert Whitehurst from Liverpool to add yet more firepower to City's attack. Such was his impact that Whitehurst finished the season as the club's record league goalscorer with 24 goals in just 15 appearances – a record that stood for 40 years. Included in Whitehurst's tally was a club-record seven goals in that 8-0 thrashing of Tranmere. Whitehurst's feat beat the five goals scored by Charlie Moore in a 9-1 win over Nelson the previous season. City's record of 128 goals beat the previous record of 127 set by Millwall in the Third Division (South) the previous season.

The recordbreaking goal was scored by Sam Barkas in the 3-1 home win over South Shields in the last match of the season on Saturday 4th May 1929. All these spectacular statistics might suggest that City's march to the Third Division (North) championship was a formality – far from it. They were pressed all the way by Stockport County, who finished in second place, only one point behind and, who, themselves, also topped 100 goals – 111, in fact. And, it needed a 16-match unbeaten run-in to the end of the season, including five consecutive away wins, to make sure of the title – only one team went up from the regional third divisions in those days.

HAT-TRICK OF TITLES

City's third championship triumph came in 1984/85 when they won the Third Division title under player-manager Trevor Cherry although, tragically, their championship success was completely overshadowed by the Valley Parade disaster on the final day of the season. The Bantams made two key signings in preparation for one of their most successful campaigns – defender Dave Evans joined from Halifax Town and winger John Hendrie from Coventry City. They only enjoyed an average start to the campaign with three wins and three defeats in their first seven matches, but a 3-1 home win over promotion rivals Millwall at the end of November – in the middle of a six-match winning run – took them to the top of the table and they never lost top spot, finishing four points in front of the London side. Unfortunately, Cherry was injured in that match and played only five more games before being forced to retire.

City were a hugely entertaining, predomantly young side, playing attacking football to the delight of their fans, but they also lived dangerously on occasions. A prime example was a home match against Brentford in March, when City went 3-0 down after 20 minutes only to win 5-4. City made sure of promotion with a 4-0 win at bottom club Cambridge United with four matches still to play – leading scorer Bobby Campbell scored two of them and the other two were scored by John Hawley. They lost their next two matches against AFC Bournemouth away, and Reading at home, but Cherry returned to steady their nerves for the May Day Bank Holiday match at Bolton Wanderers, which they won 2-0 to make sure of the championship. The players received the championship trophy before the last match against Lincoln City at Valley Parade, but the match was abandoned when fire broke out in the main stand just before half-time. City played with a remarkably settled side that season. Stuart McCall and John Hendrie were ever presents while defenders, skipper Peter Jackson, Dave Evans and left-back Chris Withe, missed only one match and winger Mark Ellis missed two. Three club records were set in that memorable season – most league wins (28), most away wins (13), and most points since three points for a win was introduced in 1981 (94).

PROMOTION YEARS

After three frustrating near misses in the seven seasons during the 1960s, City finally won promotion back to the Fourth Division in 1968/69 under new manager Jimmy Wheeler thanks to some remarkably consistent second-half form – a record-breaking run of 21 matches without defeat. The run ended with a 2-1 defeat at Brentford on the Monday night leaving City needing to win in their final match at promotion rivals Darlington on the Friday to make sure of the fourth promotion place. An 11,851 crowd packed into Feethams for a winners-takes-all match with both teams knowing that a win would take them up to the Third Division. Defeat would keep them down in Division Four. City conceded an early goal and there was a delay after the crush of spectators at the visitors' end broke down a fence. When the match restarted City set about the task of winning the match, which they duly did – 3-1 – thanks to goals from Bruce Bannister, Bobby Ham and an own goal from Tony Moor. Promotion looked highly unlikely when City lost 1-0 at home to Workington on December 28th – a match that marked the halfway mark of the season.

The Bantams had won only seven of their first 23 matches and the Workington defeat was their sixth match without a win. The revival – and the beginning of their 21-match unbeaten run – started with a 2-0 win at Notts County and there were other fine away successes like the 5-1 win at Grimsby when one of the goals was scored by a new signing, the lanky and somewhat ungainly centre forward Norman Corner from Lincoln City. A fortnight later Corner scored a hat-trick in the 3-1 win at Newport County. Corner proved to be a key signing, scoring eight goals in his 21 games and teaming up well with Bobby Ham and Bruce Bannister. Ham, the only ever present, was leading scorer with 18, including four in a 5-0 home win over York City, John Hall scored nine and Bannister seven. The team also included the 'penalty king' Charlie Rackstraw, who also notched seven goals. Despite some indifferent early season form, City had a settled side with half-backs Bruce Stowell and Tony Leighton missing only one match and centre-half Tom Hallett missing only two games while Hall played 41 matches and left-back Ian Cooper 37.

THE BASEMENT

City spent five seasons in the Fourth Division following their relegation in 1971/72 before manager Bobby Kennedy led them back to the Third Division in fourth place in 1976/77. The Bantams made a good start to the season with nine wins in their first 13 matches and led the table after beating Newport County at home on October 16th, but they sagged in mid-season with only two wins in 13 matches between November 12th and February 5th. There followed two, four-match winning runs to get the promotion drive back on track and City made sure with a 1-1 draw at home to AFC Bournemouth in the penultimate match of the season with a goal from Joe Cooke.

Cooke, who also played as a central defender, was leading scorer with 17 goals in 40 league games while left winger Don Hutchins scored 14 and new signing from Huddersfield Town, future manager Terry Dolan scored 11. Defender David Fretwell was the only ever-present and other consistent performers were goalkeeper Peter Downsborough, who missed only one match, while Hutchins missed only two matches, Dolan three while midfielder Rod Johnson made 40 league appearances. Kennedy also signed defender Phil Nicholls from Crewe Alexandra, centre forward Bernie Wright from Walsall and midfielder Alex Spark from Motherwell, to strengthen the squad. There was an interesting match early season when City drew 3-3 with Stockport County at a wet Valley Parade where Bantams centre forward Gerry Ingram and Stockport's Barney Daniels each grabbed a hat-trick. However, later that season Ingram – who scored 68 goals in 199 league and cup appearances in five years at Valley Parade after joining them from Preston – left the club for the USA to play for Washington DC. He is now an American citizen.

Roy McFarland inspired City to promotion back to the old Third Division in 1981/82 as they finished in second place, five points behind the glamour team of the Fourth Division, Sheffield United. The former England international defender, who joined City from Derby County in May 1981, transformed a group of players – who finished 19 18 in the bottom half of the division the season before – into a confident, consistent promotion side. McFarland made only two significant signings – defender Joe Cooke returned from Exeter City to share central defensive duties with the young Peter Jackson and midfielder Mike Lester, also signed from Exeter. After taking only one point from their first two matches, City equalled a clubrecord run of nine wins in a row set in 1954. The sequence began with a 6-2 home win over York City with Bobby Campbell scoring a hat-trick, and finished with a 3-2 win at Stockport County. In the process the team scored 29 goals, eight to Campbell and six to local-born wide man Barry Gallagher. Then, came the moment of truth; a home match against Sheffield United, which attracted a crowd of 13,711 to Valley Parade, City's biggest in the league for almost two years. The Blades brought City down to earth, outwitting them in a 2-0 win. It proved to be only a temporary setback, however, as City continued to show the consistency required of a promotion team, but always trailing Sheffield United. The return match at Bramall Lane came on a Tuesday night at the end of March, when a crowd of 24,593 – an extraordinarily large turnout for a Fourth Division match – saw a tense, defensively dominated contest. In a game of few chances, United went ahead, but City equalised from the penalty spot in the second half, dead-ball expert Gallagher drilling home the spot kick to give the Bantams a share of the points.

David McNiven scored all the goals in a 4-1 midweek home win against Crewe three matches from the end of the season and promotion was confirmed on the Saturday with a 2-2 home draw against Bournemouth in front of 9,768 happy fans. That left the Bantams to enjoy a promotion party with a 2-0 win at Mansfield Town in the final match. Campbell was top scorer with 24 league goals while McNiven scored 19 and Gallagher 16, six of them penalties.

TWIN TOWERS

Three months from the end of the 1995/96 season, promotion looked highly unlikely, but City won nine and lost only four of their last 14 matches to clinch the final play-off place before beating Notts County in the play-off final on a memorable day at the old Wembley Stadium. There have been many eventful seasons at Valley Parade, but this was up there with the best of them.

1996 – THE START OF THE ADVENTURE

City began the season with Lennie Lawrence in charge, but, although they enjoyed a creditable run in the League Cup with a win over Premier League Nottingham Forest before losing out to another Premier League club Norwich City, league results were disappointing. So, after they lost 2-1 at Brentford on the last Saturday in November, chairman Geoffrey Richmond decided to call time on Lawrence's 18-month spell at Valley Parade. Richmond promoted Lawrence's number two Chris Kamara to take his place and he made a winning start with a 2-1 victory over Preston North End in a second-round FA Cup tie shown live on Sky TV. Leftback Wayne Jacobs scored both goals. After that, Kamara's early league results were decidedly mixed – home wins over Peterborough United and Oxford United and away victories at York and Stockport were followed by three defeats in a row against Brighton, Bournemouth and Rotherham. A home win over Crewe and a draw at Shrewsbury were then followed by defeats against Stockport at home and Bristol City away, but, despite these setbacks, Richmond pressed on with the progress of the club. City were stuck in mid-table with promotion a wildly optimistic prospect on the day he announced the building of a new £4.5 million stand on Midland Road. However, City beat Wrexham 2-0 at home that night and soon after the race for sixth place began. One of the highlights of those last 14 matches was a 3-2 win at Burnley on Easter Saturday when Andy Kiwomya scored a last-minute winner and they followed up that notable victory by beating

Carlisle United 3-1 at home on Easter Monday. They lost 2-1 at Walsall before beating play-off rivals Chesterfield 2-1, and Brentford 2-1 at home, despite Tommy Wright and Lee Duxbury missing penalties. There followed a nervous 1-1 home draw against Swindon, which left them needing to win their final match at Hull City to make sure of sixth place. In a highly charged atmosphere, City were twice forced to come from behind before winning 3-2. Mark Stallard, Kamara's shrewd £110,000 signing from Derby County, scored the first equaliser and Duxbury the second equaliser before Carl Shutt scored the winner. It was a good job for City that they did win because rivals Chesterfield also won, but had to settle for seventh position, one place behind the Bantams. And so to the play-off semi-finals where City hugely disappointed their supporters in a near capacity 14,000 crowd at Valley Parade by losing the first leg 2-0 to Blackpool.

WHAT A NIGHT!

Only the most optimistic supporter would have given them much chance in the second leg at Bloomfield Road. However, Shutt pulled a goal back after 39 minutes and then Des Hamilton levelled the aggregate scores at 2-2 in the 68th minute before Stallard scored the winner 12 minutes from the end to put the seal one of the most memorable nights in the club's long history. And so to Wembley where 30,000 City supporters in a crowd of 39,000 saw them enjoy a relatively comfortable 2-0 win over Notts County. Hamilton gave them a seventh-minute lead and Stallard scored a second goal after 74 minutes with Ian Ormondroyd supplying the final pass just after coming on as substitute. There were joyful scenes at Wembley and the following day in Bradford where the team were given a civic reception.

THE BOARD DECIDE TO GO FOR IT...

Having consolidated their place in the old First Division – the second tier of English football – over two years since their play-off triumph at Wembley in May 1996, the City directors – Geoffrey Richmond, Julian and his father Professor David Rhodes – decided to make a determined bid to win promotion to the Premier League by investing the amounts of money in the team that would make long-standing supporters blink with disbelief. Manager Paul Jewell was given £4.3 million to spend on new players and he signed three £1 million players – striker Lee Mills for £1 million from Port Vale, striker Isaiah Rankin for £1.3 million from Arsenal, and another striker, Dean Windass for £950,000 from Oxford United, which rose by another £50,000 if the club gained promotion, which they did. Other major signings were midfielder Gareth Whalley from Crewe Alexandra for £600,000 and left-back Lee Todd from Southampton for £250,000, while right-back Stephen Wright joined them from Glasgow Rangers on a free transfer.

However, the most eye-catching signing was former skipper Stuart McCall, who rejoined the club on a free transfer from Rangers. He was given a hero's welcome on his return to Valley Parade and there was a fairytale ending as he led City to promotion as captain. Promotion was far from everyone's thoughts as City made a bad start to the new campaign and were next to the bottom of the table after the first seven matches with only five points out of a possible 21. However, they turned the corner with a 2-0 win at West Bromwich Albion and were so consistent that they lost only seven of their last 39 matches. City made sure of the second automatic promotion place in a dramatic and never-to-be-forgotten final match against Wolves at Molineux. City needed to win to be sure of finishing second, but went behind after 12 minutes when Norwegian international striker Havard Flo put Wolves ahead.

Peter Beagrie equalised after 25 minutes before leading scorer Lee Mills put City ahead five minutes before half-time after taking a pass from fellow striker Robbie Blake. Blake appeared to have made the game safe for City when he scored their third goal after 64 minutes, but there was more drama to come. The Bantams had a great chance to score a fourth when they were awarded a penalty after 77 minutes when Jamie Lawrence was brought down by former City defender Dean Richards. But Beagrie's spot kick was saved by long-serving goalkeeper Mike Stowell and Wolves made City pay for that miss three minutes later when future Carlisle, Preston, Shrewsbury and Stockport manager Paul Simpson pulled a goal back to set up a tense finish. City hearts missed a beat when Simpson's free kick hit the post five minutes from the end, but the Bantams survived to win 3-2 and earn promotion to the Premier League. It was as well that they did win because their nearest rivals Ipswich had beaten Sheffield United 4-1 to finish in third place, one point behind City. A huge crowd greeted the players when they arrived back at Valley Parade that Sunday evening and the following night people lined the streets as they rode from Keighley to Bradford on a double-decker bus for a civic reception.

CITY IN THE PREMIER LEAGUE

City's 77-year wait to play in the top division again ended when they made their Premier League debut at Middlesbrough on Saturday 7th August 1999. Boro included England international Paul Gascoigne and former Bantams goalkeeper Mark Schwarzer in their line-up. City produced a classic away performance, frustrating Boro as they soaked up pressure with a disciplined defensive display before Welsh international striker Dean Saunders, who had joined the club only 24 hours earlier from Sheffield United, struck the winning goal one minute from the end. Tottenham Hotspur were the visitors on a special day in City's history – the club's first live Premier League match on Sky TV – and what a dramatic finale there was for the TV audience. Chris Perry headed Spurs into the lead 14 minutes from the end following a corner from French international David Ginola, but City kept going and were rewarded with a headed equaliser from skipper Stuart McCall three minutes into stoppage time. The draw wasn't enough to lift City out of the bottom three, but it raised the spirits of their players and supporters after the team had lost their previous three matches.

TOP-FLIGHT WIN NUMBER TWO

City found it tough going in the Premier League and, after their opening match, they had to wait until late September before they gained their second win of the season. It came at Derby County on Saturday 25th September thanks to a 66th-minute own goal from Horacio Carbonari and an outstanding performance by goalkeeper Gary Walsh. City snatched the winner when Carbonari sliced a header into his own net as he tried to clear right-back Gunnar Halle's free kick. The Bantams were given a sharp lesson in the reality of life in the Premier League when Sunderland beat them 4-0 at Valley Parade on Saturday 2nd October 1999. Alex Rae and Irish international, now chairman, Niall Quinn put Sunderland 2-0 up before ace finisher Kevin Phillips scored two more in the last couple of minutes. The result meant that City were without a win in their first four home matches.

NO CHRISTMAS CHEER

Bradford had another lesson of how cruel Premier League life can be on Boxing Day 1999 against Manchester United at Old Trafford. City were doing well to hold their illustrious opponents to 0-0 in gruelling conditions, when United manager Alex Ferguson decided to bring on two substitutes, strikers Dwight Yorke and Andy Cole, for the last 20 minutes. The move paid immediate dividends as South African Quinton Fortune put them ahead after 75 minutes. Yorke added a second after 79 minutes, and, as City wilted, Cole scored a third on 87 minutes and Roy Keane a fourth after 89 minutes. A 4-0 scoreline did scant justice to City's battling performance. Manager Alex Ferguson confided to the City management after the match that United put games into categories A, B and C. "Unfortunately, you are Dean Saunders' Historic goal. the Welsh international striker fires City's to their first-ever Premier League win in 1999.Frank Lampard and Joe Cole, who both moved to Chelsea, went 2-1 in front through Trevor Sinclair and John Moncur only for Peter Beagrie to equalise from the penalty spot on the stroke of half-time. Jamie Lawrence then shook the home fans by scoring two goals early in the second half to establish a 4-2 lead after 51 minutes and Dean Saunders almost scored a fifth, hitting the woodwork before West Ham's revival began. A further goal at that stage would surely have ensured victory for City, but the home side pulled a goal back with a penalty from Paolo Di Canio. Joe Cole equalised before Lampard broke City's hearts by scoring the winner seven minutes from the end.

FORTRESS VALLEY PARADE

City extended their unbeaten home run to six matches with a 1-1 draw against a star studded Chelsea side at Valley Parade on Saturday 8th January 2000. The match proved to be a thriller, full of goalmouth incidents and a glut of chances for both sides. The Bantams had the perfect start when Lee Mills headed them into the lead after only 59 seconds. Future City player Dan Petrescu equalised for Chelsea, but they couldn't manage a winner despite having 36 shots on goal. Goalkeeper Matt Clarke made some fine saves while right-back Gunnar Halle cleared off the line. The visit of relegation rivals Watford on Saturday 22nd January 2000 was a must-win match for City and they duly obliged by beating their fellow strugglers 3-2. Peter Beagrie put City in front with a penalty only for Micah Hyde to equalise. City then took command by going 3-1 in front with goals from Gareth Whalley and Andy O'Brien before they lost goalkeeper Matt Clarke through injury. Deputy Aidan Davison took his place and there was a tense finale after Heidar Helgusson pulled a goal back for Watford.

SEASON HIGHLIGHT

One of the highlights of City's first season in the Premier League was a 2-1 home win over a star studded Arsenal team at Valley Parade on Saturday 5th February, 2000. Dean Windass put them in front after ten minutes direct from a free kick, but French international Thierry Henry equalised three minutes later. Dean Saunders restored City's lead after 57 minutes and they hung on to claim a famous victory.

EAST END THRILLER

City lost a 4-2 lead as they went down 5-4 in a thriller against West Ham United at Upton Park on Saturday 12th February 2000. Dean Windass headed City into the lead on the half hour, but West Ham, who included England internationals Rio Ferdinand, now with Manchester United, "I think the scoreline was a bit unfair. Bradford are a better team than last season and I think they have a genuine chance of staying up." Frank Lampard and Joe Cole, who both moved to Chelsea, went 2-1 in front through Trevor Sinclair and John Moncur only for Peter Beagrie to equalise from the penalty spot on the stroke of half-time. Jamie Lawrence then shook the home fans by scoring two goals early in the second half to establish a 4-2 lead after 51 minutes and Dean Saunders almost scored a fifth, hitting the woodwork before West Ham's revival began. A further goal at that stage would surely have ensured victory for City, but the home side pulled a goal back with a penalty from Paolo Di Canio. Joe Cole, who signed for Liverpool in the 2010 close season, equalised before Lampard broke City's hearts by scoring the winner seven minutes from the end.

EVERY LITTLE HELPS

The Bantams earned a valuable point in their battle for Premiership survival with a 1-1 draw at Tottenham Hotspur thanks to an equaliser from Jamie Lawrence three minutes before half-time. Norwegian international Steffan Iversen gave Spurs a 14th-minute lead, but they couldn't force a winner thanks to City's gritty defensive display with goalkeeper Aidan Davison making some fine saves.

ONLY LIVERPOOL TO BEAT

City crashed to a 3-0 defeat at Leicester City on Saturday 6th May 2000 to leave them facing a crucial last match at home to Liverpool in which to ensure their Premier League survival. All the goals came in the second half – two to Matt Elliott and one to Tony Cottee. The Liverpool match – on Sunday 14th May 2000 – will go down in City's history as one of the club's most memorable occasions thanks to one man, current youth-team manager David Wetherall. Wetherall, City's only ever-present in the Premier League, headed the only goal of the match from right-back Gunnar Halle's accurate free kick after 12 minutes to ensure Premier League survival against all the odds and prove the pundits wrong. Even after that excellent start most people in the big crowd at Valley Parade expected Liverpool to come back strongly because they needed a win to ensure Champions League football at Anfield the following season. However, City defended stoutly with Wetherall and Andy O'Brien in outstanding form as they managed to deny their illustrious opponents. Interestingly, the Liverpool side contained three players who were in England's 2010 World Cup squad – Steven Gerrard, Emile Heskey and Jamie Carragher.

SEASON TWO

Ironically, Liverpool were City's opponents on the opening day of their second Premier League season. Emile Heskey scored a 68th-minute winner to condemn City to a 1-0 defeat at Anfield on Saturday 19th August 2000. Earlier, goalkeeper Matt Clarke had denied Liverpool with some fine saves from Steven Gerrard, Michael Owen and Heskey as Liverpool dominated the match in front of a 44,183 crowd that included 3,000 travelling City supporters. City produced their best Premier League performance with a 2-0 win over Chelsea in the second match of the second season at Valley Parade on Tuesday 22nd August 2000, to the delight of the 17,872 crowd. The Bantams outclassed their star-studded opponents for long periods and deserved their win. They went ahead after 24 minutes and new signing Benito Carbone scored their second goal to crown a superb home debut. What a contrast was provided by City's next home match – a dour 0-0 draw at home to Leicester City on Saturday 28th August 2000 – and the Bantams also lost 21-year-old central defender Andy O'Brien with a broken collarbone. One of the highlights for the crowd came before the match when Sky TV pundit Rodney Marsh had his head shaved on the pitch after promising he would do so if City survived their first season in the Premier League.

SIX OF THE WORST

Alex Ferguson had some words of encouragement, but nothing could ease the pain of City's 6-0 thrashing against Manchester United at Old Trafford in front of a 67,447 crowd on Tuesday 5th September 2000. Andy Cole and Quinton Fortune gave United a 2-0 half-time lead and they scored four more in the second period with Fortune notching his second goal and Teddy Sheringham scoring twice before David Beckham completed the rout five minutes from the end with United's sixth goal. Ferguson said: "I think the scoreline was a bit unfair. Bradford are a better team than last season and I think they have a genuine chance of staying up."

COLLYWOBBLER

City paraded their new signing, England centre forward Stan Collymore in the West Yorkshire derby against Leeds United at Valley Parade on Sunday 29th October 2000 and he scored a spectacular goal from Benito Carbone's cross. However, Leeds denied them only their second win of the season when Mark Viduka scored the equaliser.

DEVILISH REDS

A capacity crowd of 20,552 – City's biggest for 31 years – saw Manchester United win 3-0 on Saturday 13th January 2001 to leave the Bantams at the bottom of the table, eight points adrift of safety with only 15 points from 22 matches as relegation beckoned. City matched the leaders for 72 minutes before their former United goalkeeper Gary Walsh made a bad mistake, miskicking in front of goal to leave Teddy Sheringham with an easy chance. And then the floodgates opened. Ryan Giggs added a second after a great solo run and substitute Luke Chadwick scored a third.

UNHAPPY ADDICKS

City ended a ten-match run without a win by beating Charlton Athletic 2-0 at Valley Parade on Good Friday, 13th April 2001. Robbie Blake put them in front from the penalty spot after 72 minutes after Gunnar

Halle had been fouled in the box. The second goal eight minutes from the end was a superb effort from Benito Carbone, who seized on a headed clearance from goalkeeper Sasa Ilic and lobbed the ball into the empty net. It was City's first win since they beat Leicester City away on New Year's Day.

RAMMED

The Bantams gained a rare second win in a row when they beat Derby County 2-0 at Valley Parade on Saturday 21st April 2001 to delay the inevitable relegation. Ashley Ward scored both goals against his old club with Benito Carbone producing a stirring performance. Ward gave City the lead in the first half from Stuart McCall's cross and put the result beyond any doubt three minutes from the end by deflecting Eoin Jess's shot into the net.

DOUBLE WHAMMY

Relegation was confirmed a week later with a 2-1 defeat at Everton in an eventful match, in which City missed two penalties. Andy Myers gave City the perfect start, putting them in front after two minutes, but Duncan Ferguson equalised a minute after half-time and Niclas Alexandersson scored the winner after 65 minutes. However, the result could have been different if Robbie Blake and Benito Carbone had not missed penalties.

RED REVENGE

Liverpool gained revenge for their defeat at Valley Parade the previous season with a 2-0 win on May 1st 2001. Michael Owen put Liverpool ahead after 47 minutes before Gary McAllister scored a second goal direct from a free kick 20 minutes later.

HIT FOR SIX

After drawing 1-1 with Middlesbrough in their final Premier League home match, City suffered the humiliation of a 6-1 defeat at arch-rivals Leeds United in their next to the last match. To make matters worse two players, skipper Stuart McCall and Andy Myers, had to be kept apart by their teammates after a clash in the City penalty area. It left McCall with a cut below his left eye, which needed stitches. The brawl cost both players two weeks' wages. City went 2-0 down before Ashley Ward pulled a goal back, but then Leeds scored four more goals without reply. Injury-hit City bowed out of the Premier League with their first away point for four months – a 0-0 draw at Coventry City on Saturday 19th May 2001.

TOP SCORERS

Bradford City's record scorer is David Layne, known as Bronco, who scored 34 league goals in the club's failed Fourth Division promotion bid in 1961/62. Layne had been signed for a club record £6,000 from Swindon Town by Peter Jackson midway through the previous season, but although the sharp shooter scored a creditable ten goals in 22 appearances, he couldn't save City from relegation and Jackson lost his job two months before the end of the campaign. City had a poor first half of the season under new manager Bob Brocklebank in what was their first Fourth Division campaign, but, led by Layne, they picked up well in the second half only to miss out by finishing fifth when four teams were promoted. Layne notched three hat-tricks during the season and scored 11 goals in the last six matches, but his efforts were in vain and he left during the summer to join First Division Sheffield Wednesday for a record £22,500 fee. Layne proved himself in the top division, finishing as top scorer in the following two seasons, and had scored 52 goals in 74 games when he was caught up in the match rigging and betting scandal of the mid-1960s. He was sent to jail and banned from football for life. The ban was lifted in 1972, but he couldn't resurrect his form and after failing to regain his place at Wednesday he joined Hereford United briefly on loan before going into non-league football with Matlock Town where injury brought his career to an end.

HOTSHOT MCCOLE

John McCole joined City from Scottish League club Falkirk in September 1958 and was an instant success, breaking the club's scoring record with 28 goals in 34 league matches plus six in four FA Cup ties. In that first season, McCole scored three hat-tricks; in a 7-1 win over Rochdale and a 6-1 victory against Southend United, both at home, as well as in a 4-3 win at Mansfield Town in an FA Cup first-round tie. McCole continued where he had left off when the new season began, scoring four goals in the first eight matches, but then came a surprise £10,000 transfer to neighbours Leeds United. He continued his goalscoring exploits for Leeds in the old First Division and finished the season with an impressive 22 goals. Unfortunately, for Leeds, they had a leaky defence and were relegated. After scoring 45 goals in 78 league matches at Elland Road, McCole made a surprise return to City in October 1961 and played a key role in their unsuccessful promotion bid, helping David Layne to his own record 34 league goals while scoring ten himself. McCole was the move again later that year, to Rotherham United, and later played for Shelbourne in Ireland and Newport County before returning to Ireland to play for Cork Hibernians. Sadly, he died in Ireland in 1981 aged just 45.

HE MADE HIS MARK

Rodney Green may have lacked finesse, but the bustling centre forward will be remembered for one outstanding season during his 18-month stay at Valley Parade. In that, his only complete season – 1963/64 – Green scored 29 league goals in 44 appearances as City narrowly missed out on promotion by finishing in fifth place for the second time in three seasons. Green, who joined City from his hometown club Halifax Town in January 1963, scored two hat-tricks – in a 4-2 home win against Chesterfield and 7-1 thrashing of Barrow at Valley Parade – but his efforts were in vain as City missed out on a return to the Third Division. Green had given proof of his goalscoring ability the season before, scoring ten goals in the second half of the campaign. His overall tally of 41 in 68 league and cup appearances was impressive by any standards. It was inevitable he would leave Valley Parade following City's failure to gain promotion, but at least they received a £7,000 fee for him when he was transferred to Gillingham in the summer of 1964.

CAMPBELL'S KINGDOM

Belfast-born Bobby Campbell became a cult figure among City supporters during two spells at the club during the 1980s. He arrived at Valley Parade in January 1980 with a 'bad boy' image having been sacked by Halifax Town for breach of club discipline. He had also been banned by the Northern Ireland FA as a 17-year-old for taking part in a 'joyride' during a tour of Switzerland. When he left City for the second time in October 1986 he had written his name into the club's history books as one of the most popular players of all time with 137 league and cup goals in 310 appearances. He was a great character and much loved by the fans. Campbell had been playing in Australia for Brisbane City following his departure from Halifax when he first appeared at Valley Parade. He was initially given a month's trial by manager George Mullhall, but such was the interest from other clubs that City felt obliged to offer him a longterm contract and he did not disappoint. The strong, bustling, no nonsense centre forward scored eight goals in 21 appearances in his first season before establishing himself as leading scorer in the next three campaigns. He scored 22 league and cup goals in 1980/81 and he continued to thrive under new player-manager Roy McFarland as he scored 27 goals in the 1981/82 promotion season, and 30 in 1982/83. McFarland persuaded the Northern Ireland FA to lift their ban on him in 1982 and he played a full international against Scotland before making a substitute appearance against Wales at the end of City's 1981/82 promotion season.

He also went to Spain for the World Cup in 1982, but was never fit to play. Then came a dramatic turn of events; Campbell was sold to Derby County for £70,000, by receiver Peter Flescher, in the summer of 1983 to ease City's financial problems. Less than five months later he was back at

Valley Parade scoring goals. He was leading scorer with 23 league goals and three in the FA Cup in the Third Division championship season of 1984/85 and, although he scored only ten goals in 41 league appearances following promotion to the old Second Division, he was still a key part of the team. Manager Trevor Cherry sprang a surprise by selling Campbell to Wigan Athletic two months into the 1986/87 season for £25,000, bringing in Mark Leonard from Stockport County as a replacement – a decision seriously questioned by many supporters. Campbell played two more seasons, scoring 27 league goals in 69 appearances, mainly as a striking partner for future City player and manager Paul Jewell, before retiring. He began his career as an apprentice at Aston Villa and, while he was at Villa Park, had a loan spell at Halifax before being transferred to Huddersfield Town and then Sheffield United. He returned to Huddersfield and also had a spell in Canada playing for Vancouver before returning to Halifax. However, it was at Valley Parade where he enjoyed most success. In all, he made 476 league appearances, 274 of them with City, scoring 179 goals, 121 of them for the Bantams for whom he also scored 16 cup goals in 36 appearances.

TO BE FRANK

The robust, bustling Scottish centre forward Frank O'Rourke played for City in their most successful period – the seven years leading up to World War I. O'Rourke – no relation to Peter O'Rourke, the manager, who signed him – joined the Bantams in April 1907 from Airdrieonians and was top scorer in three of the next four seasons. He missed only two matches in his first full season when he was leading scorer with 21 goals in 36 games as City won promotion to the First Division as Second Division champions in 1907/08. He played just as important a role in keeping the club in the top flight the following season. The only player to appear in every match, O'Rourke was again top scorer with 19 goals in 38 league matches, including six in the last six games, including a priceless goal in their 1-0 win over Manchester United in the final game of the season that ensured survival. He was second-top scorer with 20 goals the following campaign and leading scorer again in 1910/11 with 13 goals in 32 matches as City achieved their highest-ever placing – fifth in the top division – as well as winning the FA Cup. O'Rourke's appearances began to tail off after that, but after retiring from first-team football during World War I, he continued to captain the reserve side into his 40s, playing at centre-half. He continued to work for the club as first-team trainer when his playing days were over before returning to his birthplace Bargeddie in 1926 after 19 years' impressive service to the club. O'Rourke established a record of 88 league goals in 192 appearances that stood for 69 years before it was broken by Bobby Campbell in 1984. He also scored five goals in 20 FA Cup matches.

SEAN MCCARTHY

To average one goal in every two matches is the aim of every striker and that was the superb strike rate that Sean McCarthy achieved in three-anda- half seasons at Valley Parade. Bridgend-born McCarthy, who began his career at Swansea City, joined City from Plymouth Argyle in the summer of 1990 in a £250,000 deal, new manager John Docherty's star signing as he looked to build a promotion team following relegation from the old Second Division. Although City failed to achieve their objective during his spell at the club, that was not McCarthy's fault. He scored 60 goals in 131 league matches and was leading scorer in each of his four seasons at Valley Parade. McCarthy's strong, sturdy build not only enabled him to score goals himself, but also create chances for others. One player to benefit was his striking partner and future manager Paul Jewell. They formed an effective partnership, their best season being in 1992/93 when they scored 33 goals between them – 17 for McCarthy and 26 for Jewell. McCarthy made a great start to the 1993/94 season with 14 league goals in the first 18 matches and seven in the League Cup as City thrashed Darlington 11-1 in a two-legged tie. Not surprisingly, McCarthy began to attract attention from other clubs and was transferred to Oldham Athletic, then managed by Joe Royle.

The reported £500,000 deal involved young striker Neil Tolson coming to Valley Parade. It was later revealed that City received only £350,000 from the deal, who clearly overvalued Tolson, who didn't measure up as an adequate replacement for McCarthy. The truth was that City were desperate to sell to pay an urgent debt. It says a lot about the rest of the team that, although McCarthy left City at the end of November, he still ended the season as leading scorer with 14 league goals, and seven in the League Cup. McCarthy spent three-anda- half years at Oldham, scoring 42 goals in 140 league matches, before continuing his career at Bristol City, Plymouth Argyle for a second spell and Exeter City. In a career spanning 16 years, McCarthy made 544 league appearances, including 69 as substitute, scoring 172 goals.

LITTLE HAM, BIG GOALSCORER

Bradford-born Bobby Ham, who enjoyed two spells at Valley Parade, was a natural finisher. Not particularly tall, he played well off taller strikers, adept at picking up loose balls and converting them into goals. Ham averaged a little better than one goal in every three matches, scoring 70 league and cup goals in 208 appearances for the club. He also scored regularly at his other clubs with 53 league goals in 159 appearances in two spells at Bradford Park Avenue, 24 league goals in 67 matches at Preston North End, and 24 league goals in 67 appearances at Rotherham United. He also scored one goal in two appearances at Grimsby Town, giving him a total of 156 league goals in 456 appearances spread over 14 years. Ham, who played for City as a junior, established himself as a league player with Park Avenue, enjoying his best season in 1965/66 after forming a prolific partnership with highly-rated Kevin Hector, who went on to enjoy an illustrious career with Derby County as well as winning two England caps.

Despite being the most marked striker in the Fourth Division, Hector scored 44 goals that season, while Ham playing alongside him netted 22. Ham was transferred from Park Avenue to City in February 1968 in a £2,500 deal and helped them to win promotion from the Fourth Division the following season. Although he spent most of his career in the lower divisions, Ham almost joined Tottenham Hotspur in January 1970 after catching the eye of manager Bill Nicholson when City played Spurs in the FA Cup third round. Spurs offered £35,000 plus a player, but City rejected this offer much to the disappointment of Ham, who described it as his biggest disappointment in football. He left City to go to Preston North End in October 1970 and helped them to win the Third Division championship. He then played for Rotherham United before manager Bryan Edwards signed him for City. After being released by the Bantams in 1975 he joined non-league Gainsborough Trinity, but suffered a double fracture of the leg that finished his football career. He then took up rugby union and played for Cleckheaton and Baildon until he was 52. He became a City director after the 2004 administration crisis, helping with commercial activities, but left to help the revival of non-league AFC Halifax Town after they were demoted three divisions when they got into serious financial difficulties.

FIRST OF THE BIG SPENDERS

Lee Mills was Bradford City's first £1 million player when he joined from Port Vale just before the 1998/99 season and proved to be a key player, top scoring with 23 league goals as City won promotion to the Premier League. Born in the South Yorkshire town of Mexborough, Mills began his Football League career at Wolverhampton Wanderers and moved to Derby County before settling at Port Vale where he scored 35 league goals in 109 appearances, 28 of them from the bench. Manager Paul Jewell signed him for City in August 1998 and he enjoyed an outstanding season at Valley Parade, forming a fine understanding with his striking partner Robbie Blake. Mills was not the most skilful of players, but he was a good finisher inside the six-yard area. But, he couldn't command a regular place once City gained promotion to the Premier League. He had a brief spell on loan to Manchester City before he was transferred to Portsmouth just before the start of City's second Premier League season having scored 28 goals in 65 league appearances. He later played for Coventry City and Stoke City before moving into non-league football.

DEANO, DEANO!

Dean Windass – a natural goalscorer, with a sharp eye for a chance and the ability to make room for himself in any goalmouth – enjoyed two successful spells at City, scoring 76 league goals in 216 appearances, plus nine in 23 FA and League Cup matches. His association with the club began in March 1999 when he joined from Oxford United in a £950,000 move with the promise of another £50,000 if the club gained promotion to the Premier League, which they duly did two months later. That made him City's third £1 million player in less than 12 months. Two years later, with the Bantams facing relegation from the Premier League, Windass left Valley Parade for Middlesbrough in a £600,000 deal. He returned to the club after a spell at Sheffield United and enjoyed his best season in 2004/05 after the club were relegated to League One. He scored 28 goals in that campaign and 20 more the following season. In fact, he was so successful he was top scorer in four successive seasons after returning to City from Bramall Lane. The club sprang a surprise by allowing him to rejoin his home town club Hull City on loan in January 2007 – a move that became permanent the following summer – and he helped the Tigers gain promotion to the Premier League for the first time in their history at the age of 39. It was a proud moment for Windass, but he was left out by manager Phil Brown once Hull were in the Premier League and spent a brief spell on loan at Oldham Athletic before teaming up as an assistant to his former City manager Colin Todd at Darlington in 2009. Unfortunately, bad results at the start of the season cost both of them their jobs and since then Windass has worked for Sky Sports. Windass originally joined Hull from Hull district non-league club North Ferriby and scored 57 league goals in 176 appearances before joining Aberdeen.

FAR FROM AVERAGE

Albert Whitehurst played a mere 43 league and FA Cup matches in a twoyear spell, but what a goals-per-match ratio he enjoyed during his two-year spell at Valley Parade. He joined City from Liverpool in February 1929 with the Bantams strong favourites to win the Third Division (North) championship. Whitehurst made sure they did as he scored a remarkable 24 goals in only 15 matches, including seven goals in an 8-0 home win over Tranmere Rovers, four goals in the following match, another 8-0 thrashing this time against Barrow also at Valley Parade. Whitehurst also scored a hattrick in a 5-0 home win against Wrexham a fortnight later. After playing a crucial part in City's promotion, Whitehurst must have been disappointed to make only 15 league appearances, scoring six goals when City returned to Division Two. His City career petered out in the following campaign with a mere eight appearances and no goals. In fact, he made four appearances late in the campaign at right-half. So, it was no surprise that he left City in the 1931 close season, when he joined Tranmere Rovers before retiring on medical advice in 1933. Whitehurst, who also played with Stoke City and Rochdale, claimed 184 league goals. Who could forget his astonishing first three months at Valley Parade and his remarkable goalscoring feats?

HARD-SHOT HALLOWS

Jack Hallows was a consistent goalscoring centre forward for six seasons when City established themselves as a decent Second Division side in the early 1930s. His tally of 74 league goals in 164 matches places him in fourth place behind Bobby Campbell, Frank O'Rourke and Dean Windass in the club's list of all-time goalscorers. City signed Hallows from Kent League club Grays Thurrock in November 1930 for £600 and what a bargain he turned out to be. Hallows, who had a hard shot, was an immediate success, scoring 19 goals in 27 league matches in his first season and 21 in 34 games in his second season. His personal high point that season came when he scored five goals as City hammered Barnsley 9-1 in January 1932. However, his goals began to tail off in his final two seasons at Valley Parade and a two-month suspension imposed by the club after he was sent off in a reserve match restricted him in his final season. After scoring 79 league and FA Cup goals in 173 appearances for City, he was transferred to Barnsley in March 1936, but he couldn't repeat his goalscoring form at Oakwell and made only 13 appearances, scoring four goals before retiring. After his football career was over, Hallows began a bespoke tailoring business in the Bolton area. He died in August 1963.

SNOWED IN

David McNiven looked to be an exciting prospect when he joined City from Leeds United for £25,000 in February 1978. The Scottish schoolboy and under-21 international striker joined Leeds in 1972 when the team that manager Don Revie created was still one of the top three sides in England. In the face of fierce competition from established internationals, McNiven had to wait until 1976 for his league debut, scoring a goal against Manchester City after coming on as substitute. However, despite being a prolific scorer for United's junior and reserve sides, he failed to gain a regular first-team place at Elland Road. By the time he arrived at Valley Parade, he had made only 20 league appearances spread over five years. Nonetheless, there were high hopes that he would be a huge success in third division football. Speed off the mark allied to a good finish appeared to be the answer to City's dreams as they battled to survive in the third tier. McNiven made a dream start putting City in front on his debut at Plymouth, but the match was abandoned after a blizzard drove the players off the field after 61 minutes. In fact, the weather was so bad that all roads around Plymouth were closed and the City players and officials had to stay the night before travelling home by train the following day.

However, McNiven scored on what can only be described as his full debut the following Saturday in a 3-0 home win over Rotherham that gave City hope of avoiding relegation. But, they won only four of their remaining 17 matches to the end of the season and were relegated 12 months after gaining promotion from Division Four. The match at Plymouth was re-arranged for the last match of the season and City, who were by then already relegated, crashed 6-0, leaving supporters to wonder what might have been if the match three months earlier had not been abandoned. McNiven scored five goals in 18 matches in his first season and was leading scorer for the next two seasons – 15 goals in 1978/79 and 17 in 1979/80 when City finished in fifth place, missing out on promotion on goal average. His tally dipped to eight goals in 1980/81, but he enjoyed an outstanding season in 1981/82 when City gained promotion from the Fourth Division under player-manager Roy McFarland. A small, somewhat stocky, but quick striker, McNiven was the perfect foil for the strong and competitive Bobby Campbell and their partnership was a crucial element in City gaining promotion. They scored 43 league goals between them with Campbell netting 24 and McNiven 19, including in City's 4-1 home win over Crewe just before the end of the season. McNiven didn't do as well the following campaign and three months after he succeeded McFarland as player-manager, allowed him to leave. So, he joined Blackpool on a free transfer in February 1983 and then had a spell in the USA with Pittsburgh Spirit before returning to England to join Halifax Town and ending his career with then non-league Morecambe. McNiven made 245 league and cup appearances with City, scoring 66 goals, 64 of them in the league.

SMASH AND GRAB

Sharp and clever in and around the penalty area, Bradford-born Bruce Bannister was a goalscoring opportunist who averaged roughly one goal in every three games at his two main clubs, Bradford City and Bristol Rovers. Bannister, who made his City debut as an 18-year-old in September 1965, scored 68 league and cup goals in 228 matches over a six-year period before leaving for Bristol Rovers in 1971 for a club-record £23,000. There he enjoyed a successful five-year spell, scoring 80 league goals in 206 appearances, striking an outstanding partnership with Alan Warboys – they became known as 'Smash and Grab'. After leaving Bristol Rovers, Bannister continued his career at Plymouth and Hull before moving to France to play for US Dunkerque. His eye for goal brought him 167 league goals in 523 matches for his four English clubs over 14 seasons and he said: "Nothing can take away the thrill of scoring a goal and I have that thrill even now after my career is over. Speak to any forward and you will get exactly the same response – just knocking the ball over the line causes this ridiculous thrill." After his football career was over, Bannister established a successful business – Sports Shoes Unlimited – in Bradford.

STARTING YOUNG...

Joe Cooke alternated between centre-half and centre forward during his 16-year career, but still managed to score more than 100 league and cup goals. Born in Dominica, Cooke came to Bradford as a child and was one of the early black players to make his mark in English football. He made his debut as a 16-year-old in September 1971 and scored 62 league goals in 204 matches in his first spell at Valley Parade. City used him as a centre forward in 1975/76, when they reached the FA Cup quarter-final and he scored 22 league goals in 42 appearances. He also played a key role the following season, when City gained promotion from Division Four, scoring 17 league goals in 40 matches, including the goal that earned them a top-four place in a 2-2 home draw against AFC Bournemouth. City sold him to Peterborough United for £45,000 in January 1979 and he later played for Oxford United and Exeter City before player-manager Roy McFarland brought him back to Valley Parade in a £10,000 deal in January 1982 to play a key role as a central defender in the run-in to promotion from Division Four. He left in 1984 and played for Rochdale and Wrexham, being captain at both clubs before retiring in 1987. His career record with City was 79 goals in 302 league and cup appearances.

INSPIRED SWITCH

City had a potential centre-forward problem when John McCole was unexpectedly transferred to Leeds United for £10,000 in mid-September with the 1959/60 season only eight matches old. McCole had scored 28 league goals the previous campaign, plus six in the FA Cup, and his would be big boots to fill. However, manager Peter Jackson switched Derek Stokes from outside-left to centre forward and not even he could have imagined how successful this positional change would turn out to be. Born at Normanton, Stokes, who joined City as a 16-year-old from West Yorkshire junior club Syndale Road Athletic in 1956, showed his goalscoring ability the season before – 1958/59. Then, he scored 15 goals in 45 league appearances and one in the FA Cup despite playing every game on the wing. However, his career took off in a spectacular way the following season when he scored 25 in the league and ten in City's memorable eightmatch FA Cup run that took them to the fifth round before they were knocked out by Burnley 5-0 in a replay at Turf Moor after they scored a stoppage-time equaliser to draw the first match 2-2. Unfortunately for City, Stokes missed the last nine matches through injury and it was a sign of how much they depended on him that they scored only seven goals in that spell without him in the side. After scoring 35 league and cup goals that season, it was inevitable he would be on the move and neighbours Huddersfield Town signed him that summer for £20,000. Stokes enjoyed six successful seasons at Huddersfield, scoring

63 goals in 153 league matches despite having his career there disrupted by two years' National Service in the RAF. His goalscoring record also earned him international recognition and he played four times for the England under-23 team. His return to City in January 1966 was a popular move with supporters, but Stokes could not repeat his goalscoring form second time around and he left 11 months later, after scoring 11 goals in 32 appearances, to join the Irish club Dundalk where City teammate, central defender Alan Fox, had been appointed player-manager. He helped Dundalk to win the league and cup double in his first season and played in the old Fairs Cup for three years before leaving Ireland to return to England and try his hand at non-league management in West Yorkshire with Fryston Colliery Welfare. His record with City was 66 league and cup goals in 141 appearances, and his career total was 121 goals in 278 Football League appearances, not including his appearances with Dundalk.

SAVIOUR GERRY?

When City signed Gerry Ingram from Preston North End just before transfer deadline day in March 1972, there were high hopes that the Hullborn centre forward would solve the club's problems as relegation to the Fourth Division beckoned. Ingram arrived at Valley Parade in a deal that also brought his Preston teammates with him; left-back John Ritchie as part of a £20,000 transfer deal, along with winger David Wilson. Unfortunately, the new players made no difference to City's impending fate as the Bantams finished bottom of Division Three. Nonetheless, the blond striker enjoyed a profitable five-year career at Valley Parade, scoring 68 league and cup goals in 199 appearances as he enjoyed a twoyear striking partnership with Allan Gilliver, and then Bobby Ham. In City's first season back in the Fourth Division, 1972/73, the pair scored 35 league and cup goals between them – Gilliver 20 and Ingram 15 – but City finished a disappointing 16th and the highlights came in the FA Cup. There, Ingram had the satisfaction of scoring both goals in the 2-1 home win over his old club Blackpool before City lost 2-0 against Arsenal in front of a 40,407 crowd at Highbury. The Ingram/Gilliver partnership was also successful the following season with Ingram top scoring with 18 league and cup goals while Gilliver scored 12 as City again reached the FA Cup fourth round while finishing eighth in the league. Ingram helped City reach the quarter-final of the FA Cup in 1975/76 when they were beaten 1-0 at home by the eventual winners Southampton in front of the Match of the Day cameras and scored nine more goals in the following campaign as the Bantams won promotion back to the Third Division. He left before the end of the season to play in the United States with Washington Diplomats and settled in America when his playing days were over. So, he was lost to English football at the age of 29, but he could look back with satisfaction on a league record of roughly one goal in

every three matches – 117 in 317. After playing in non-league football on Humberside, Ingram got his big break when Blackpool paid £1,000 for him to Hull Brunswick in 1967. Such was his success at Blackpool – he scored 18 in his first full season – that neighbours Preston signed him a year later for £27,000 and he played a big part in their promotion to the Second Division in 1970/71 with 22 goals, which made him the joint top scorer in the Third Division that season.

A THORNE IN EVERY TEAM'S SIDE

One of new manager Stuart McCall's first signings when he took over at Valley Parade in the summer of 2007 was proven goalscorer Peter Thorne from Norwich City. Thorne had had his injury problems at Norwich, but McCall gave him the chance to resurrect his career with City and he was top scorer in each of the next two seasons, 15 in 2007/08 and 17 the following season. A natural finisher, Thorne had the happy knack of pulling away from his marker and finding space in the most crowded of penalty boxes. Unfortunately, knee problems restricted him to only five starts in his final season and new manager Peter Taylor released him in March 2010, a month after he took over from McCall, and he retired leaving himself three short of 200 career goals. After spells at Blackburn Rovers and Wigan Athletic, Manchester-born Thorne moved to Swindon Town where he scored 27 goals in 177 league appearances, but he really made his name at Stoke City where he scored 65 league goals in 158 matches before moving to Norwich City. Less caution, more goals Twin son of manager Peter Jackson, David Jackson scored 68 league and cup goals in 275 appearances during his six years at Valley Parade between 1955 and 1961. He admits his job as inside-forward – attacking midfielder in modern football language – was of goal provider; his goalscoring record compares with modern midfielders. Jackson, who had a strong shot and was prepared to have a go at goal, said: "I played inside-right, and John Reid inside-left, and although we scored a smattering of goals we were mainly providers. I suppose the difference between then and now is that we were less cautious. Nowadays, everyone is frightened of making mistakes." Goals from the flanks John Hendrie was a pacy goalscoring winger, who joined City on a free transfer from Coventry City in the summer of 1984 and played a key role in the Third Division championship-winning team in his first season at the club. The Scottish youth international had the ability to cut in from the wing – usually from the right – and shoot with either foot. He also played several matches as a striker and scored 59 league and cup goals in 212 appearances in his four-year spell at Valley Parade. His two most productive seasons were in 1986/87 and 1987/88 when he scored 17 league and cup goals. He left City in June 1988 after the club failed to gain promotion to the top division, being beaten in the old Second Division play-off semi-finals by Middlesbrough, and joined

Newcastle United in a £500,000 deal. He later played for Leeds United, Middlesbrough and Barnsley where he was player-manager for a season before retiring.

WINGING IN TO GOAL

Another goalscoring winger was Bobby Webb, who scored 67 league and cup goals in 233 appearances during seven seasons at Valley Parade. Born at Altofts in West Yorkshire, Webb joined Leeds United when he was 15 and played in their successful Northern Intermediate League sides and the Central League team, becoming a part-time professional while continuing to work as a miner. However, he made only three first-team appearances after making his debut in March 1954. United gave him a free transfer in March 1955 and he joined Walsall. After only four months at Walsall, Webb signed for City in July 1955 during manager Peter Jackson's first close season and he turned out to be one of his many successful signings, playing mainly on the right wing, but occasionally as an inside forward. Webb, who played most of his career as a part-timer, was top scorer in his first season with 18 league goals and contributed a steady stream of goals during his successful spell with the club. He left Valley Parade in June 1962 to sign for Torquay United, but after one season he was forced to retire after breaking his leg when he was still only 29.

LOYAL SERVANT

A speedy winger, John Hall gave 12 years of fine service to City – his only Football League club – between 1962 and 1974 and, despite playing virtually all his games on the right wing, he scored 72 league and cup goals in his 474 appearances, 63 of them in the league. His best season was in 1966/67 when he was top scorer with 17 goals from 44 league appearances. After leaving City, Hall played with a variety of non-league clubs, including Gainsborough Trinity in the Northern Premier League, Guiseley in the Yorkshire League and Leeds Ashley Road before becoming playermanager of Yeadon Celtic in the West Riding County Amateur League. Moore is more Charlie Moore began his football life as a centre forward, but played most of his 368 league and cup matches for City as a half-back, scoring 60 goals, most of them in the early part of his 13-year spell at Valley Parade. Born at Worksop, Moore joined City from Manton Colliery in October 1926 as an inside-forward and converted to centre forward the following season and was leading scorer with 17 league and cup goals, including five in City's 9-1 win against Nelson. However, he made only 14 league appearances the following campaign when City won the Third Division (North) championship as the club signed other goalscoring forwards and eventually made a significant contribution as a reliable and hard-working half-back. Moore continued to play regularly in

City's Second Division years and then, when they were relegated back to the Third Division, until the outbreak of the war. He made 42 appearances in wartime football before retiring.

FAR FROM A WALLY

Wally Smith was one of City's first goalscoring favourites, averaging one goal in every two matches during his four seasons at Valley Parade. Although he was born in Bradford, Smith moved with his family to Northamptonshire when he was a child and began his football career with Kettering Town. He enjoyed an impressive goalscoring record over three years with them before leaving to join Northampton Town, then a Southern League club, in 1904. City signed him a year later for £50 and he was an immediate success, being leading scorer in each of his two seasons – 24 league and cup goals in 1905/06, and 14 the following season. Smith formed a productive striking partnership with new signing Scottish international Frank O'Rourke, and they played a big part in City's Second Division championship triumph in 1907/08, scoring 41 goals between them, but his goals dried up in the First Division and, after failing to score in 16 appearances in the top flight, he was transferred midway through the season to Leicester Fosse for £750. Leicester were relegated to Division Two at the end of that season and Smith moved to Hull City. Injury forced Smith to retire in 1912 and he died at his home in Worksop in 1917, aged only 34. Smith's record with City was 58 goals in 120 league and cup appearances, including 20 league goals in the 1905/06 and 1907/08 seasons.

BOB LIKES PLAYING AGAINST LONDONERS!

He stayed with City only 15 months, but Bob Whittingham established a record of the most goals scored by a player in the top division. The insideright, who joined the Bantams from Blackpool in January 1909, was top scorer with 21 league goals – one more than Frank O'Rourke – in 1909/10 before leaving for Chelsea three matches before the end of the campaign. His tally included two hat-tricks against Tottenham Hotspur and Chelsea, whom he joined just over a week later.

JOHN MCMILLAN

The top scorer in City's first season was skipper John McMillan with 14 goals. McMillan, one of City's first signings from Small Heath – now Birmingham City – scored 27 league and cup goals in 91 appearances before leaving for Glossop North End in 1906.

HIGHEST CROWDS

City's highest-ever crowd came during their path to the FA Cup Final in the 1910/11 season, when 39,146 turned up to watch them beat Burnley

1-0 in the quarter-final. It is the longest-standing home ground record in the Football League. Following modern safety regulations and the introduction of all-seater stadia after the Hillsborough disaster in 1989, all ground capacities have been reduced. Ground changes and safety measures reduced Valley Parade's capacity to just over 16,000 in the 1980s, but following the rebuilding after the 1985 fire, the addition of a new Midland Road Stand in 1996, and the extension of the main stand in 2001, the present capacity is 25,000.

FIRST RE-ELECTION

The club's highest post-war crowd came in the 1948/49 season when 27,083 packed into Valley Parade to see a struggling City side excel themselves by beating Hull City, then the Third Division (North) glamour team 4-2. Hull, parading player-manager, former England inside-forward Raich Carter, were expected to win but Scottish centre forward Jimmy Brown scored a hat-trick and Frank Greenhoff scored the other goal as City caused a huge upset. Unfortunately for the Bantams fans, it was an all too rare success and they were forced to apply for re-election for the first time in their history.

LOWEST CROWDS

The club's lowest crowd was for the final match of the 1980/81 season when a mere 1,249 turned up to watch a 1-0 defeat against Hereford United. It was a disappointing end to a disappointing season – a hangover from the previous campaign when City missed out on promotion by losing the last match at Peterborough United. The situation wasn't helped by the fact that the match was rearranged two weeks after the previous match – a 3-0 win at York. Among the crowd was Derby County's England international defender Roy McFarland, who had been offered the player-manager's job. Despite the depressing atmosphere at Valley Parade that night, McFarland accepted the club's offer and led City to promotion the following season.

I DON'T LIKE MONDAY NIGHTS

The season City reached the FA Cup quarter-final before being beaten 1-0 at home to the eventual winners Southampton ended on a flat note when their first-ever sub-2,000 crowd turned up to watch the final home match of the season – a Monday night fixture against Newport County. The stayaways missed a rare win for since their quarter-final defeat the team won only three of their next 15 league matches, but at least they ended the season on a high note with a 3-0 victory, two of them scored by young Clive McFadzean in only his third match.

CITY'S FINEST HOUR

Undoubtedly City's greatest cup triumph came in 1911 when they lifted the FA Cup for the only time in their history, beating Newcastle United 1-0 in a replay at Old Trafford after the first match at Crystal Palace had ended goalless. A crowd of 66,464 crammed into Old Trafford for the replay and City delighted their 10,000 supporters by taking the lead after 15 minutes through skipper Jimmy Speirs. Newcastle goalkeeper Jimmy Lawrence dashed out of his goal to collect the ball, but was distracted as centre forward Frank O'Rourke rushed towards him. The ball slipped past him and Speirs was credited with getting the last touch as the ball rolled into the empty net. That was the end of the scoring as City's strong defence, superbly marshalled by Bob Torrance, kept the normally free-scoring Newcastle attack at bay. Thousands packed into Bradford city centre as the players brought home the cup. City made a spirited attempt to retain the FA Cup the following season before being knocked out in the quarterfinal by Barnsley, who went on to win the trophy for the only time in their history. The cup campaign began well with a 4-0 home win over Queens Park Rangers in a replay after the first match had ended goalless.

New signing Harry Walden scored a hat-trick and Peter Logan scored the other goal. Dickie Bond and Peter Logan scored the goals that enabled City to beat Chelsea 2-0 at home in the next round to set up an away tie at Bradford Park Avenue. A goal by Frank O'Rourke settled a tense, frantic match in City's favour and set up a quarter-final at Barnsley. In those days, City had one of the best defences in the league and, after not conceding a goal in their first three cup matches, the first two matches against Barnsley – first at Oakwell and then at Valley Parade – ended goalless, as did a second replay at Leeds City's Elland Road ground. A fourth replay was needed to settle the tie. This time Sheffield United's Bramall Lane ground was chosen and a crowd of 38,264 gathered for what turned out to be an epic match full of drama. Goals from Jimmy Speirs and Archie Devine gave City a 2-1 lead with a minute of normal time to go, but Barnsley equalised to send the match into extra time, and then broke the hearts of City supporters by scoring a dramatic winner with one minute of extra time remaining.

ALMOST A DOZEN

City's biggest FA Cup win came in a first-round replay against the northeast based non-league side Walker Celtic at Valley Parade in the 1937/38 season. There was no sign of the drubbing to come when the first match ended 1-1, but City ruthlessly cast aside their opponents in the replay the following Wednesday afternoon – no floodlights in those days – by thrashing them 11-3. The prolific Jack Deakin, who scored the goal in

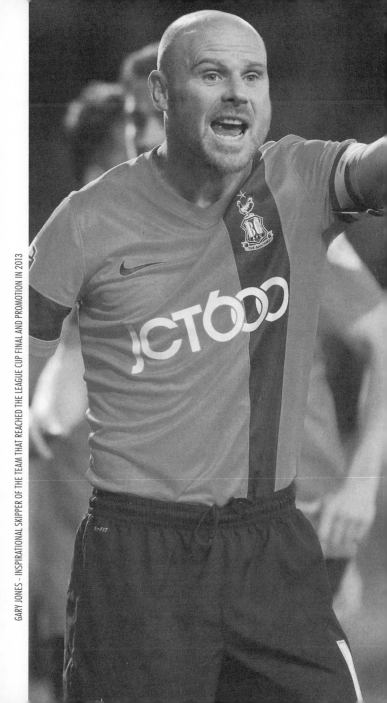

the first match, scored four – one a penalty – as did Roland Bartholomew. The other goals were scored by Tom Bagley, Alf Whittingham and William Cooke in front a crowd of 4,770. Other non-league clubs to suffer a drubbing at Valley Parade were Fleetwood and Tow Law Town. City thrashed Fleetwood, then in the Lancashire Combination, 9-0 in the first round in the 1949/50 season. Experienced strikers, Eddie Carr and Bill Price shared seven of the goals, Carr scoring four and Price three, one of them a penalty. Andy McGill and Polly Ward scored the other goals. The 7-2 win against Tow Law Town from the north-east was a triumph for Don Goodman. Goodman – who later played for West Bromwich Albion, Sunderland and Wolverhampton Wanderers – scored a hat-trick within 14 minutes of coming on as a substitute. Other scorers were Bobby Campbell (2), Stuart McCall and John Hendrie. Fixture-'computer' fate Like most league clubs, City have also had their share of humiliations in the FA Cup. One of the biggest was against Midland League club Worksop Town in a second-round tie in the 1955/56 season. City were somewhat fortunate as they came from behind to draw 2-2 at Valley Parade to earn a replay before going out 1-0 in the replay the following Thursday. By a strange quirk of fixtures, City reserves who, in those days, played in the Midland League, then went to Worksop two days later for a league match and beat the team who had knocked the first team out of the cup.

UNEXPECTED KNOCKOUT

For consistent results, City have enjoyed few better seasons than the Third Division championship campaign in 1984/85, but they were surprisingly knocked out of the FA Cup third round 2-1 on a frozen pitch at non-league Telford United. It was a rare setback in an otherwise memorable season.

NOWHERE NEAR CLOSE, AND CERTAINLY NO CIGAR

Since they won the FA Cup in 1910/11, City have never been close to repeating the feat. The nearest they have come has been three quarter-final appearances – in 1911/12, 1919/20 and 1975/76. The season after City won the cup – 1911/12 – Barnsley knocked them out of the competition in the most dramatic of circumstances after three replays, before going on to win the cup for the only time in their history. The first match was goalless, as was the first replay at Valley Parade, and the second replay at Elland Road, which meant that City had conceded only one goal in the FA Cup in 14 matches spread over two seasons. However, the third replay at Bramall Lane was a dramatic affair. Goals from Jimmy Speirs and Archie Devine put City 2-1 ahead with one minute to go, but Barnsley equalised and then broke City hearts by scoring the winner in the last minute of extra time.

TOO MANY CHOCS AWAY

In 1919/20, the first season after the war, City, then still a First Division club, beat Portsmouth and Sheffield United at home and Preston North End away to reach the FA Cup quarter-final with an away tie at Bristol City. It was a match they were expected to win, but they went down to a 2-0 defeat with contemporary commentators tending to blame an illadvised trip to a chocolate factory on the morning of the match for their disappointing result.

A VERY GOOD RUN

In 1975/76, City, then a lower-half Fourth Division club, surprised the football world by reaching the quarter-final before being beaten by the eventual winners Southampton, 1-0 at Valley Parade in front of a 14,195 crowd. City enjoyed a smooth passage to the fifth round, beating Chesterfield at home, Rotherham United and Shrewsbury Town away and non-league Tooting & Mitcham at home before facing a difficult draw at Norwich City, then a First Division club. The match was delayed for ten days owing to a flu epidemic in Bradford. Don Hutchins put City in front after 38 minutes, but Norwich equalised through World Cup winner Martin Peters two minutes later. The tie was heading for a replay, when Scot Billy McGinley, a former Leeds United and Huddersfield Town reserve striker, equalised three minutes from the end. Match of the Day cameras made a rare appearance at Valley Parade for the quarter-final, but there were no more cup shocks as Southampton won a tight match 1-0 before going on to beat Manchester United in the final.

FULL HOUSE AT TURF MOOR

City's second-best post-war FA Cup run came in the 1959/60 season when they reached the fifth round before being knocked out 5-0 by Burnley in a replay at Turf Moor. The cup run spanned eight matches, including three replays. They began by beating Barnsley in the first round after a replay. The first match at Oakwell ended in a 3-3 draw, but City won the replay 2-1. The second round against Rochdale also went to a replay. They drew 1-1 at Rochdale before beating them 2-1 at home to set up a third-round tie against Everton – a Third Division team against a side from the old First Division. City gained a surprisingly comfortable 3-0 win in front of a 23,550 crowd. They then beat Bournemouth – a club from their own division – 3-1 at home in the fourth round to set up a home tie against Burnley, then one of the leading teams in the country. A capacity crowd of 26,227 came to see the tie in muddy conditions and City fans were delighted as the Bantams established a 2-0 lead through Bobby Webb and Derek Stokes with 15 minutes to go. Unfortunately for them, Burnley pulled a goal back and then equalised in stoppage time with a scrambled effort after City had failed to clear a corner. That was City's last chance of an upset for, in the replay, Burnley went 2-0 up after five minutes and won the match 5-0 in front of a capacity 52,850 crowd with an estimated 20,000, many of them from Bradford, locked out. A feature of City's cup run was the form of centre forward Stokes, who scored ten goals in eight matches.

MCCOLE FLYING

The previous season – 1958/59 – City did well to reach the fourth round before being cruelly knocked out 3-2 at Deepdale by Preston North End, then a First Division club. The cup run had begun with a thrilling 4-3 win at Mansfield Town in the first round thanks to a hat-trick by John McCole and another goal by David Jackson. McCole scored both goals in a 2-0 win at Bradford Park Avenue in the second round. However, City's hopes of a lucrative third-round tie against a leading club were dashed when they were drawn away to Brighton & Hove Albion. However, they gained a creditable 2-0 win even though goalkeeper Geoff Smith was injured and played as a passenger on the right wing – there were no substitutes in those days – and goalscoring hero of the previous two rounds, John McCole, went in goal. City's scorers were David Jackson and Derek Stokes. An even more difficult tie at Preston beckoned in the fourth round, but City were leading 2-1 at one stage with goals from McCole and Jim Lawlor, but conceded a last-minute equaliser when they failed to clear a corner. Their only consolation was a share of gate receipts from a 35,716 crowd.

VILLA TOPPLED

Perhaps City's best FA Cup result between the wars came in a third-round tie at Aston Villa. City were then struggling in the Second Division and were given little chance of beating First Division Villa, but they excelled themselves, coming out on top 3-1 with goals from Charles Keetley (2) and the prolific centre forward Jack Hallows. Unfortunately, City came down to earth in the next round when Third Division (North) side Stockport County knocked them out 3-2 after extra time in a replay. The first match at Valley Parade ended goalless.

STOWELL AND EDWARDS SPUR A REPLAY

Two of the most memorable post-war cup ties to be staged at Valley Parade involved Tottenham Hotspur. Spurs, playing with their famous strike force of England's Jimmy Greaves and Scotland's Alan Gilzean, came to Valley Parade in January 1970 for a third-round tie in front of a 23,000 crowd and quickly went 2-0 up with Greaves scoring one of the goals. At that stage, a Spurs win looked to be a formality, but City hit back to level the scores before half-time with goals from Bruce Stowell and an

own goal from Welsh international defender Mike Edwards. There were no more goals although City winger John Hall was lucky to see his shot headed off the line ten minutes from time by left-back Cyril Knowles and Spurs thrashed the Bantams in the replay at White Hart Lane 5-0.

MAGIC FROM MITCHELL

Spurs' second FA Cup visit to Valley Parade came again in a third-round tie in January 1989 when City won 1-0 thanks to a goal from Scottish right-back Brian Mitchell three minutes before half-time in front of a 15,917 crowd. Mick Kennedy's quickly taken free kick surprised the Spurs defenders and Mitchell's low, right-foot shot from the edge of the penalty area eluded visiting goalkeeper Bobby Mimms.

A WADDLE WONDER

One of City's best away results in the FA Cup in modern times was at Everton in the 1996/97 season. City won this fourth-round tie 3-2, but the match will always be remembered for a superb goal by former England winger Chris Waddle. His 40-yard chip shot, which soared over the head of Welsh international goalkeeper Neville Southall to give City a 2-0 lead in the 51st minute, is rated as one of the best goals in FA Cup history. Waddle spotted Southall off his line and chipped he ball over his head. After a goalless first half, defender John Dreyer put City in front after 47 minutes and, although Everton pulled a goal back three minutes after Waddle's superb effort through an own goal from Andy O'Brien, Swedish striker Rob Steiner put City back in control with their third goal after 60 minutes. Everton scored their second in stoppage time, but it was too little, too late. Manager Chris Kamara said: "The scoreline flattered Everton. We outplayed them."

STARS OF 1911

One newspaper commentator spoke of City's team showing Yorkshire grit in winning the FA Cup against Newcastle United in 1911. In fact, the team comprised eight Scotsmen, one Irishman and two players who were born in Nottinghamshire.

THE LURE OF THE 'SOUTH'

The captain of that team – and scorer of the all-important winning goal in the Old Trafford replay – was Glasgow-born Jimmy Speirs. A goalscoring inside forward, Speirs played with Glasgow Rangers and Clyde before manager Peter O'Rourke tempted him south in the summer of 1909 to join City. Having survived their first season in the First Division by the narrowest of margins, City needed some team strengthening and Speirs was a key part of the process masterminded by fellow Scot Peter O'Rourke. Speirs was a great success in his first season, being an ever-present with 38 league appearances and scoring six goals. However, it was the following season that he wrote his place in City's history. He scored seven goals in 25 league appearances as City achieved their highest-ever placing – fifth in the top division, seven points behind champions Manchester United – but it was the FA Cup that provided Speirs with his finest hour. Speirs, then 25, was not only captain of the side that lifted the cup for the only time in City's history, but he scored the winning goal in the cup final replay and proudly received the coveted trophy before leading the victory parade in a packed Bradford city centre later that evening. Speirs played only ten times the following season, scoring seven goals, and in December 1912 he moved to Leeds City for £1,400 – a sizeable fee at a time when the average wage was £2 a week and the top players earned £4. In three-and-a-half seasons at Valley Parade, Speirs scored 33 goals in 96 league and cup matches. League football continued in the first year of the war before it was suspended in May 1915 when it was realised there would be no early end to the hostilities and Speirs scored ten goals in 25 appearances in what proved to be his last season. Speirs joined the Queen's Own Cameron Highlanders and after being promoted to lance corporal while training at Inverness, he was posted to France where he was promoted to corporal. In May 1917, Speirs was awarded the Military medal for 'bravery in the field'. He gained further promotion as the leadership qualities he showed on the football field were recognised by the military authorities and in June 1917 he was promoted to sergeant. Speirs went home to Glasgow in the July, but he returned to France and was killed at the Battle of Passchendale in the August.

THE RED KNIGHT OF KIRKINTILLOCH

Bob Torrance, a surprise selection for the replay at the heart of the defence, turned out to be one of City's cup-winning heroes. Known as the Red Knight of Kirkintilloch, Torrance joined City in the 1907 close season and played initially as a full-back, but couldn't gain a regular place in the side. However, his career took off after the final replay when he impressed with a strong defensive performance that shut out the normally free-scoring Newcastle side. He became a regular in the side after the cup triumph, making 179 league and cup appearances spread over eight seasons as well as playing in 52 wartime matches, but, like Speirs, he was killed in action in World War I. He joined the Royal Field Artillery as a gunner and was wounded in action at Ypres in Belgium in April 1918. Just over six months before the war ended, he lost an arm after his unit was hit by shelling and died a few days later when a field hospital where he was a patient was shelled. He has no known grave.

LOGAN'S GOOD RUN

Peter Logan, who deputised in the final for the suspended outside-right Dickie Bond, joined City from the Scottish junior club Edinburgh St Bernard's in October 1908 and made 304 league and cup appearances, scoring 43 goals spread over 17 years either side of World War I as well as playing 67 wartime matches. Logan, whose brother Jimmy was also on City's books for 18 months in 1905 and 1906, was a versatile forward player, who operated on both wings and the two inside-forward positions. All but one of his seasons at Valley Parade were spent in the First Division.

FULL-BACKS OF A DIFFERENT GENERATION

The two full-backs were Robert Campbell and David Taylor, both Scots. Right-back Campbell was born at Lugar Boswell and played with Partick Thistle and Glasgow Rangers before moving to London in 1905 to play Southern League football with Millwall Athletic. After one season there, he moved to City and won a Second Division championship medal two years later, but clearly, winning the FA Cup with the Bantams was the highlight of his nine-year career at Valley Parade. Nowadays, we are used to seeing full-backs run down the flanks and cross the ball or even cut in and have a shot at goal. That didn't happen in Campbell's day, when fullbacks were primarily defenders, whose job it was to clear the ball upfield, and there was no-one better at doing that than Robert Campbell. City fans cheered when he made one of his famous hefty clearances over the halfway line. Campbell was a member of City's first touring party to the Continent and was a popular figure with his hosts. In fact, the Belgians nicknamed him 'L'aime' ('the friendly one') because of his constant smile. Away from football, Campbell was a keen angler and played league cricket in Scotland as a professional. He retired during World War I having made 247 league and cup appearances, and scoring just one goal. David Taylor, left-back in the cup-winning side, was born at Bannockburn and joined City from Glasgow Rangers in October 1910. He became a regular in the side, playing first at centre-half and then at left-back, missing only one league match after making his debut at Sunderland. He missed only one of City's seven cup matches on their way to an Old Trafford replay. However, Taylor's stay at Valley Parade proved to be short and he was transferred to Burnley the following December for a four-figure fee and won a second FA Cup winners' medal when the Clarets lifted the trophy in 1914. He later managed St Johnstone.

NEARLY TWO DECADES

Other Scots in the side were fearless centre forward Frank O'Rourke, halfback Jimmy McDonald and inside-forward Archie Devine. O'Rourke, who joined City from Airdrieonians and shared in two triumphs during his

19-year spell at Valley Parade – the FA Cup win and the Second Division championship – scored 93 league and cup goals in seven years as a first-team regular before playing reserve football and then becoming first-team trainer.

ANOTHER SCOT

A skilful ball-winning half-back, Jimmy McDonald was one of City's most influential players before World War I after joining from Edinburgh St Bernard's and, like O'Rourke, a regular in the Second Division title and FA Cup-winning sides – he left the club in 1920, returning to Scotland with Raith Rovers after a 13-year spell at Valley Parade. Archie Devine signed from Falkirk in April 1910, a year before the cup win, and played 60 league and cup matches over three years, scoring 11 goals before being transferred to Arsenal. Devine, who also played for Raith Rovers and Hearts before joining Falkirk, returned to Scotland when his playing days were over and became a docker in Glasgow.

ENGLISHMEN IN YORKSHIRE

Half-back George Robinson, one of only two Englishmen in the cup-winning side, played in City's first-ever match and made 377 league and cup appearances spread over 11 seasons, before becoming first-team trainer. The other Englishman in the cup final team was goalkeeper Mark Mellors. Like Robinson, Mellors, a tall, handsome man with an elegant moustache, was born in Nottinghamshire and joined City in March 1909 from Sheffield United for £350 when the club was battling against relegation during their first season in the top division. He turned out to be another inspired signing by manager Peter O'Rourke for he was the hero of the final match against Manchester City in front of 30,000 at Valley Parade. City knew they had the chance of escaping relegation if they could beat Manchester City that April evening and centre forward Frank O'Rourke put them in front in the second half. However, near the end Mellors was knocked out as he dived to save and was propped up in goal as City defended the resulting corner. City defended desperately and resolutely as they managed to hang on to their lead and they survived while Manchester City were relegated. Mellors was carried off the pitch shoulder high by delighted City supporters. The goalkeeper made 82 league and cup appearances in four seasons in the first team before retiring at the end of World War I and going into business as a successful wool merchant.

SCOTSMEN, ENGLISHMEN AND AN IRISHMAN...

The only Irishman in the 1911 FA Cup Final side was outside-left Frank Thompson, who joined City from Linfield in April 1910 and made 60 league and cup appearances, scoring 13 goals in a three-year career with the club before he was transferred to Scottish League club Clyde.

LEAGUE CUP HIGHLIGHTS

One of City's best results in the League Cup before 2013 came in the first season of the competition. A visit from Manchester United is normally a huge event in the life of a Third Division club, as City were in November 1960, but the Bantams had scrapped their first floodlight system and had not yet installed new ones. So, the match had to be played on a Wednesday afternoon in daylight. Consequently, only 4,670 saw this famous 2-1 win. City's scorers were former Huddersfield Town reserve winger Gerry Smith and Bobby Webb. Smith only played 11 league and cup games for City, but this was his moment of glory. The Bantams came back to earth in the next round, going out 2-1 at Shrewsbury Town.

A TREBLE, BUT NO DICE

City, by then relegated to the Fourth Division, hosted another top side two seasons later –1961/62 – when Aston Villa visited Valley Parade, but this time there was no happy outcome. Villa won a thriller 4-3 as Bobby Webb scored a hat-trick for City, but finished on the losing side. Seven Villans The Bantams also met Aston Villa in the League Cup three years later, but this time at Villa Park, Villa put an end to City's remarkable five-match run, all five of them away from home. The League Cup run bore no relation to City's poor league form – they needed to win their last two matches to avoid having to seek re-election. City's League Cup run began with a 2-0 home win over York City, followed by a remarkable 5-3 victory at Exeter City where John Hellawell scored a hat-trick and Dudley Price scored the other two goals. They then beat Doncaster Rovers 2-1 away to set up a tough away match at Charlton Athletic. Few people gave them a chance, but Hellawell scored the only goal of the match to give them a memorable win. It was Hellawell's fifth goal in City's cup run. However, City met their match at Villa in the next round as they were thrashed 7-1 with Price scoring the consolation goal.

ROCKED AT THE ROKER

City have had few better League Cup results than their 2-1 second round win at First Division Sunderland. The Bantams, full of confidence after gaining promotion from the Fourth Division the season before, had reached the second round by beating Chesterfield over two legs to set up a trip to the old Roker Park ground. There, goals from Bruce Bannister and Norman Corner earned them a memorable win. Then, after beating Southend United 2-1 at home in the next round, their run ended in emphatic fashion at West Bromwich where they crashed 4-0.

KING KENNY

A League Cup tie that will always stick out in the minds of many City supporters was the two-legged second-round encounter with Liverpool in the 1980/81 season. City had earned their matches against Liverpool by beating Rotherham United over two legs in the first round and they shocked the top First Division side, then at the height of their powers, by beating them 1-0 to the delight of Bradford supporters in the capacity 16,233 crowd. The only goal came 11 minutes from the end from Bobby Campbell, who drove the ball into the net after Liverpool had failed to clear Terry Dolan's free kick. That goal gave City a 1-0 lead to take into the second leg at Anfield, but it wasn't enough as Liverpool, strengthened by the return of key striker Kenny Dalglish, beat City 4-0.

EUROPEAN TEAM OF THE YEAR NICK IT

City's romance with the League Cup continued the following season – 1981/82 – with a memorable third-round tie against Ipswich, who were then managed by the late Bobby Robson. City, then managed by Roy McFarland, earned a trip to Portman Road by beating, first Blackpool in the first round, and then Mansfield Town over two legs in the second round. Few people gave City a chance at Ipswich, then one of the leading teams in the country and voted European Team of the Year the previous season, but an equaliser from Garry Watson earned them a replay at Valley Parade. The replay turned out to be a thriller, but, unfortunately for City, Ipswich edged home 3-2 after extra time.

Billy Ingham and a penalty from Barry Gallagher scored for City. City also had a high profile third-round League Cup tie the following season – this time against Manchester United. Again, City had to win two two-legged first-round ties – against Mansfield Town and Rochdale – to earn their place in the third round where they faced United at home. City put in a strong defensive performance in front of a near capacity 15,568 crowd to earn a lucrative replay at Old Trafford a fortnight later. However, the match was dominated by events off the field. For, two days before the replay, player-manager Roy McFarland and his assistant Mick Jones had walked out on the club to be part of a new look management team at their old club Derby County, leaving Bryan Edwards and chief scout Maurice Lindley in caretaker charge. There was to be no fairytale at Old Trafford as Manchester United raced into a 3-0 lead in the first 20 minutes and ran out 4-1 winners with Bobby Campbell scoring the consolation goal in front of a 24,507 crowd.

HOMELESS

A little bit of history was made when City, newly promoted to the old Second Division, played in the League Cup – by then it was called the Milk Cup – in October 1985. It was the first match that City played at Bradford's Odsal Stadium, the home of Bradford Northern Rugby League Club. City were forced to play their home matches there, as well as at Leeds United's Elland Road ground and Huddersfield Town's Leeds Road ground, after Valley Parade was devastated following the fire disaster that claimed 56 lives. City had begun the season playing home matches at Leeds and Huddersfield while the stadium's owners, Bradford Council, hastily made the ground ready for league football. However, they made their bow at Odsal, when Brighton & Hove Albion beat them 2-0 in a second round, second leg match. It completed a 7-2 aggregate triumph for Brighton, who had beaten City 5-2 in the first leg at the old Goldstone Ground.

CATALOGUE OF VICTORIES

Odsal staged three more League Cup matches the following season – by this time Littlewoods had taken over the sponsorship of the competition. They gained a creditable 2-0 win over Newcastle United in the first round, first leg with goals from Greg Abbott (penalty) and Don Goodman. And, although they lost 1-0 in the second round at St James' Park a fortnight later, they went through to the second leg 2-1 on aggregate. They then beat Portsmouth 3-1 with more goals from Goodman and Abbott, again from the penalty spot, as well as Ian Ormondroyd. The crowds for Newcastle (6,384) and Portsmouth (4,885) were disappointing, but a third round tie against Nottingham Forest, managed by Brian Clough, captured the public imagination and 16,009 crowded into the stadium. Forest were then near their peak under Clough and gave City a ruthless lesson in finishing as they ran out 5-0 winners. Afterwards, Clough, ever caustic in his comments, had a pop at the far from ideal conditions at Odsal, saying he could not understand why the ground curled up at the corners!

TWO ON THE TROT

City reached the League Cup quarter-finals twice in successive seasons – 1987/88 and 1988/89. In 1987/88 City had a team prepared for promotion to the old First Division. Unfortunately, the team slipped up in the final week of the season, lost the chance of automatic promotion and ended up in the play-offs where Middlesbrough beat them in the semi-final over two legs. They also had an excellent run in the League Cup, beginning with a remarkable 7-2 aggregate first-round win over Fulham, including a 5-1 victory at Craven Cottage in the first leg. There followed a 1-0 win at Charlton Athletic, then playing at Crystal Palace, and a win over Reading

NAHKI WELLS - BERMUDA INTERNATIONAL, WHO BECAME A PROLIFIC SCORER AND A KEY PART OF THE TEAM THAT REACHED THE LEAGUE CUP FINAL AND PROMOTION IN THE SAME SEASON

– City beat them 1-0 in a replay at Valley Parade after the first match had been goalless. That win earned them a quarter-final tie at Luton Town, but the team failed on the big occasion and went out 2-0.

MCCALL'S BACK

The highlight of City's League Cup campaign in 1988/89 was their comprehensive 3-1 home win over Everton, which marked the return to Valley Parade of Bantams' favourite Stuart McCall, who joined the First Division club the previous summer. It proved to be an unhappy 'homecoming' for McCall as City established a 2-0 lead through Mark Leonard and Ian Banks. The Bantams then killed Everton's hopes with a superb third goal scored by midfielder Leigh Palin 12 minutes into the second half, leaving Everton with a consolation goal five minutes from the end, scored by defender Dave Watson. The win took City into the quarter-final against Third Division Bristol City at Valley Parade – a match most home supporters in a bumper 15,330 crowd expected them to win. Unfortunately for City, Bristol City took the lead 90 seconds into the match through midfielder Alan Walsh and it proved to be the only goal of the match as the visitors, led by 37-year-old player-manager, Joe Jordan – the former Leeds United, Manchester United and Scotland striker playing at the back that night – frustrated the Bantams with some strong defensive work.

NEUTRAL GROUNDS

Until recent years – and before penalty shoot-outs – FA Cup ties were played until they were decided by open play. This meant as many replays as it took to settle the ties – and it also meant playing replays on neutral grounds after the first replay.

CAPITAL PUNISHMENT

City visited Arsenal's Highbury ground for the first time for 33 years thanks to the neutral grounds rule. The Bantams, who were struggling in the bottom half of Division Three (North) in season 1954/55, managed to reach the third round for the first time since the 1939-45 war. However, instead of drawing a club from the top division, they had the misfortune to be drawn away to Third Division (South) team, Brentford. It was a tough draw with no great financial reward, but they managed to earn a replay in 1-1 draw thanks to a last-gasp equaliser from Ken Lambert in front of a 12,120 crowd. The replay was played at Valley Parade on a Wednesday afternoon in January – floodlights were still a year away – and a crowd of 7,963 saw the match end in a 2-2 draw after extra time. Will Robb and Martin Bakes were the scorers. The clubs tossed a coin for the choice of a neutral ground for the second replay, Brentford won the toss and the match was played at Highbury in front of a crowd of only 5,951 and Brentford won 1-0.

THE BANNISTER AND CORNER SHOW

City had no better luck when they had to play a third replay at a neutral ground in the 1970/71 season. After beating the then non-league Macclesfield Town far from convincingly 3-2 at home in the first round, they were drawn away to Lincoln City where goals from Bruce Bannister and Norman Corner earned them a 2-2 draw and a replay at Valley Parade. The same two players were on the mark when the replay also ended 2-2 after extra time and the FA ordered the second replay to take place at Doncaster Rovers' Belle Vue ground – roughly midway between Bradford and Lincoln. In the event, City were soundly beaten 4-1 in front of a crowd of 3,296 on the Monday night before Christmas.

STRANGE CUP TIE

One of the strangest FA Cup matches in which City have taken part was a third-round replay against Norwich City on March 3rd 1915 during World War I. City beat Darlington and Middlesbrough to earn a thirdround match against Norwich City at Valley Parade, but the tie ended in a 1-1 draw after extra time. The replay at Carrow Road the following Saturday was also drawn – 0-0 – after extra time and so a second replay was arranged the following Wednesday afternoon at a neutral venue – Lincoln City's Sincil Bank ground – a specially organised condoned midweek match. To comply with the Government's wartime regulations, the match had to be played behind closed doors because they did not want people working on essential wartime projects – like munitions – being distracted by attending football matches. Although only officials and press reporters were supposed to attend, it was reported that 1,300 managed to gain admission, reportedly by climbing the fences, and they saw City win 2-0. Dickie Bond scored from the penalty spot and Jimmy McDonald scored the other goal. After all that, City lost 2-0 at home to Everton in the next round the following Saturday in front of a 26,100 crowd.

BRANDON BLOCKED

When City were drawn away to north-east non-league club Brandon United in the FA Cup first round in November 1979, the FA stated that their Northern Alliance League ground could not stage the match. There was nothing more than a perimeter fence separating the playing area from the crowd so, despite protests from Brandon, the FA ordered that a neutral venue be found to stage the match. So, the match was played five miles away at Spennymoor United's Brewery Field ground and a 5,083 crowd saw City win 3-0 with goals from Barry Gallagher, Terry Dolan and David McNiven. The club invited Brandon officials to be their guests in the next round – when City returned to the north-east where they beat Darlington 1-0, but the cup run came to an end with a 3-2 defeat to Carlisle United in the third round.

THE FUTURE

After the fire in which 56 people died wrecked Valley Parade in May 1985, City were forced to play away from their home ground for 18 months while a decision was made regarding their future venue, and rebuilding. City played 'home' matches at Leeds United's Elland Road ground and Leeds Road, then the home of Huddersfield Town, while Bradford's Odsal Stadium was made ready for their use. Even then, bad weather and clashes with Bradford Northern's matches caused the club to play more matches at Leeds and Huddersfield. It is fair to say the club were not happy playing on a rugby league ground, but it was important for the supporters' sake that City staged 'home' matches in Bradford. It was a tall order for a promoted or newly promoted club not to have a ground of their own, but despite having to play away from Valley Parade, City finished a creditable 13th in the Second Division. One of the most memorable matches at Odsal for City supporters came in September 1986 when they achieved a rare win over Leeds United. Bobby Campbell and Don Goodman were the scorers in their 2-0 win, but the match will also be remembered for an incident just before the end of normal time. Some United supporters overturned a chip van on the terracing, causing a potentially dangerous incident. The referee took the players off the field and everyone wondered what would happen. Would the match be abandoned or would play continue? The players were off the field for half an hour and most of the 13,831 crowd had left the ground by the time the referee brought them back to play out the remaining two minutes.

GOAL RECORDS

Bradford City supporters must have known that 1928/29 was going to be a special season when they thrashed Rotherham United with a record 11-1 win in their first match – and they were right. For, this amazing victory set the tone for a memorable season in which they won the Third Division (North) championship with a record number of 128 goals for a 42-match programme. New boy Trevor Edmunds from Aberdare scored a first-half hat-trick as City led 7-0 at the interval, and another new signing, Cornelius White from Bangor City, completed his hat-trick in the second half. Harvey and Aubrey Scriven twice, and Ralph Burkinshaw, completed the scoring. City also had two consecutive 8-0 wins that season. Apart from the 11-1 triumph, City's previous record victory was 9-1 against Nelson, also in Division Three (North), the previous season. The Bantams also beat Barnsley 9-1 at home on January 2nd 1932 in the Second Division with Jack Hallows scoring five, and enjoyed a 7-0 home win over Port Vale the following season with Stan Alexander scoring a hat-trick.

BOURNEMOUTH BASHED

In more modern times, they beat Bournemouth 8-1 at home on January 24th 1970 after leading 6-0 at half-time with Bobby Ham scoring a hattrick. Two years later they beat Darlington at home 7-0 on December 23rd 1972 with Gerry Ingram scoring four, including two penalties.

BIG DEFEATS

Big away defeats include an 8-0 thrashing at Manchester City on the last day of the 1926/27 season when they finished bottom of Division Two, and a 9-1 defeat at Colchester United on December 30th 1961, four days after they beat the same side 4-1 at home in a Boxing Day fixture.

TOP APPEARANCES

Ces Podd holds the club record for the number of appearances. The fullback, born on the Caribbean island of St Kitts, made his debut as an 18-year-old in the 1970/71 season and was City's regular right-back for the next 14 years, making 502 league appearances, scoring a mere three goals and playing 30 FA Cup matches and 34 in the League Cup. Podd holds a unique place in Bradford's sporting history and in the affections of City supporters. Not only does he hold the all-time club record for his number of league appearances, but he is also one of the finest ambassadors for the game itself and a role model for black and white footballers alike. A slim, athletic player with a lovely smile, Podd was one of the first black players to gain a regular place in league football. He smiled his way through the game and conducted himself in a dignified manner, even when he suffered verbal abuse. He said: "As far as I was concerned colour did not apply, but I think it hindered my progress. I was 9st 6lb and 5ft 10in when I made my debut at City, I looked bigger than I was because I was slim. In those days, back in the 1970s and 1980s, there was a doubt about whether black players were up to the physical side of the game. "That made me all the more determined. I wanted to win everything." Podd has seen the condition of black players improve considerably since he made his City debut in 1970. He said: "Every club in the league has got at least one player, but there should be more black managers and coaches." Podd was a student at the Bradford College of Art when one of his fellow students, City supporter Mick Illingworth, wrote to Valley Parade suggesting the club offer him a trial and, after completing his college course, he was signed as a professional by manager Jimmy Wheeler. Podd experienced highs and lows in his 14-year Valley Parade career as City shuttled between Third and Fourth Divisions, experiencing relegation in 1971/72 and 1977/78 and promotion in 1976/77 and 1981/82, besides appearing in an FA Cup quarter-final against Southampton at Valley Parade in March

1976. Another highlight was his testimonial match in March 1981. The fact that nearly all the black players in the league came to Bradford to support him speaks volumes about the respect Podd commanded. He lost his place in 1984 to a young Greg Abbott and joined Halifax Town, where he made 57 appearances in two years before moving to Scarborough as assistant to future Sheffield United, Crystal Palace and Queens Park Rangers manager Neil Warnock, and he helped them to win promotion to the Football League before retiring. Since then, Podd has been involved with the Football in the Community programme at Leeds United, helping with coaching at the club's academy and setting up coaching schemes around the Leeds area. He has also managed the national team on his home island of St Kitts, and has worked for a football agency in Yorkshire, as well as teaching salsa dancing.

KEEPING IT LOCAL

Three local-born players, Ian Cooper, John Hall and Bruce Stowell, have also made more than 400 league appearances. Only Podd has made more matches for the club than Bradford-born Cooper, who was a consistent defender for his hometown club for 12 seasons between 1965 and 1977 after making his debut while he was still an amateur. He made 443 league appearances, mainly at left-back, and played in 50 cup matches. Such was his consistency that Cooper was an ever-present in four seasons – 1967/68, 1970/71, 1971/72 and 1972/73 – and held the club's appearance record until it was broken by Podd. He was appointed club captain in 1972/73 and made 154 consecutive appearances between August 1970 and November 1973.

JOHN HALL

Third in City's all-time appearance stakes is pacy winger John Hall, who made 430 league appearances and played in 44 cup matches, scoring 72 league and cup goals in 13 seasons at Valley Parade. He was an ever-present in 1972/73 before leaving in 1974 and moving into non-league football.

BRUCE STOWELL

Bradford-born Stowell is fourth in the appearance list making 401 league appearances, plus 36 in the FA Cup and League Cup in a 12-year firstteam career after making his debut in April 1960, and broke the club's 55-year-old appearance record when he made his 344th appearance in October 1970. He surprisingly left City in 1972 on a free transfer and joined Rotherham United. However, he made only 16 appearances for the Millers before moving to Australia to join the Sydney club Pan Hellenic. The move to Australia opened a remarkable career as a player, coach and manager at club and national level.

A LOYAL SERVANT

George Robinson held City's appearance record for 55 years. One of City's first signings, Robinson joined the Bantams from Nottingham Forest and played in their first match at Grimsby Town in 1903. His career spanned the club's most successful period up to the outbreak of World War I. He captained City to the Second Division championship in 1908 and was vice captain when they achieved their highest-ever placing, fifth in the top division, and for the FA Cup triumph of 1911. Robinson, who played right-half, made 377 league and FA Cup appearances – 343 in the league, 34 in the cup – between 1903 and 1915. The war brought his long career to an end, but he returned to the club as trainer in 1919 and held that position until he left after their relegation from the First Division in 1922.

300+

Three modern-day players who have achieved the 300 league appearance mark are Stuart McCall, Peter Jackson and Wayne Jacobs. Leeds-born McCall, City's most popular post-war player, made 395 league appearances in two spells at Valley Parade. The iconic Scottish international midfielder joined the club as a 16-year-old in 1980 and made his debut in a home match against Reading two years later. He made 238 league appearances in midfield over six seasons before leaving to join Everton in June 1988, a month after City were beaten in the Second Division play-offs. After two years at Everton, he moved to Glasgow Rangers where he won league and cup honours, as well as playing regularly in Europe in a golden era for the club under Walter Smith. He also won 40 Scotland caps. City fans understood McCall's reasons for leaving the club to fulfil his ambitions to play top-flight league football when he could not achieve it at Valley Parade, but longed for him to return. Well, they got their wish in June 1998, ten years after he left the club, when chairman Geoffrey Richmond and manager Paul Jewell brought him back to lead the club's drive for Premier League status. McCall was made captain and he led City to promotion after an unforgettable final match of the season at Wolves. McCall stayed for four seasons before being released by manager Nicky Law in 2002, having made 157 more league appearances to add to the 238 he made in his first spell, but not before he made an emotional farewell at a memorable testimonial match against his old club Rangers at Valley Parade. Some 10,000 Rangers fans travelled to Bradford that Sunday afternoon in an amazing demonstration of support for one of their most popular players. By that time, McCall was approaching his 38th birthday, but he was by no means ready to call time on his playing career and he joined Sheffield United as player-coach. He made 71 more league appearances over the next two seasons before becoming assistant manager. He returned to City as manager in 2007.

Defender Peter Jackson also played in two spells at Valley Parade, making a total of 336 league appearances with 29 goals. Jackson signed for City as an apprentice in 1979 and played alongside two former England internationals, Roy McFarland and Trevor Cherry, during his first spell at Valley Parade. He was an inspirational captain of the 1985 Third Division championshipwinning side and was presented with the championship trophy on the day of the Valley Parade fire disaster where 56 people lost their lives. He got his big move in October 1986 when he joined Newcastle United for £250,000 and was chosen as Player of the Year in one of his two seasons at St James' Park. Jackson was tempted back to City in September 1988 in a £290,000 deal, but the move was not a success and he left two years later on a free transfer to join Huddersfield Town. He enjoyed a successful four-year spell at Huddersfield, making 155 league appearances before concluding his career with two years at Chester City having made 551 league appearances and scoring 38 goals.

Left-back Wayne Jacobs joined City on a free transfer in the summer of 1994, one of new manager Lennie Lawrence's first signings, and he went on to give 11 years of loyal service, making 318 league appearances, weighing in with 12 goals, before leaving the club in 2005 to become assistant player-manager at Halifax Town. During that time he shared in City's promotion to the Second Division through the play-off final at Wembley in 1996, and promotion to the Premier League two years later. He returned to Valley Parade as assistant to new manager Stuart McCall in 2007 and continued as number two to Peter Taylor when he succeeded McCall in February 2010.

CONSECUTIVE APPEARANCES

Left-back George Mulholland held the club record for consecutive league appearances, playing 231 times between August 1953 and September 1958 – 246 when FA Cup matches are included. City have made few better free transfer signings than Mulholland, who joined them on a free transfer from Stoke City in July 1953. A model of consistency, he made 304 league and cup appearance in a seven-year spell between 1953 and 1960 before returning to his native north-east to finish his league career at Darlington.

CHARLIE BICKNELL

The previous record was held by right-back Charlie Bicknell, who didn't miss a single match during his near-six years at the club. He made 224 league appearances between his debut, a 3-2 home win over Charlton Athletic, after joining City from Chesterfield, and his last appearance for the club – home to Doncaster Rovers on March 14th 1936. After helping City beat Doncaster Rovers 3-1, Bicknell was transferred to West Ham

United and enjoyed an 11-year career at Upton Park. Unfortunately, World War II dramatically affected his appearance tally and he only managed 149 run-outs during his time in east London. He saw out his playing career as player-manager at non-league Bedford Town.

KEIGHLEY KEEPER

Keighley-born goalkeeper Geoff Smith, a teammate of Mulholland, made 200 consecutive appearances between April 1954 and October 1958 and such was his consistency that he was an ever-present in four seasons: 1954/55, 1955/56, 1956/57 and 1957/58. The run of consecutive appearances began with the last match of the 1953/54 season at home to Gateshead and ended at Reading in October 1958. Smith made 26 league appearances that season before retiring. In all, he made 270 league and FA Cup appearances in a six-year career at Valley Parade. Smith, who played with Lancashire Combination clubs Rossendale and Nelson before joining City, also went 18 matches in season 1957/58 without conceding a goal and kept 70 clean sheets during his career. He recalls: "I was an amateur when I got into the first team at City, still working as a wagon driver. I gave up the lorry-driving job, which earned me £4 10s (£4.50) for £10 a week plus a £4 bonus for a win as a footballer, which was a good deal." Sadly, he died in 2013.

PETER DOWNSBOROUGH

Another consistent goalkeeper was Peter Downsborough. He was an ever-present in his first full season at Valley Parade – 1974/75 – and missed only three matches the following season, one in 1976/77, and was an ever-present in 1977/78. In all, the former Halifax Town keeper made 252 league and cup appearances in seven years at Valley Parade after joining them from Swindon Town in 1973 and kept 66 clean sheets.

NEAR EVER-PRESENT

Winger John Hendrie missed only one match during his four years at Valley Parade. The Scot joined City on a free transfer from Coventry City in June 1984 and what a bargain he proved to be. He was an everpresent for three seasons – 1984/85, 1985/86 and 1986/87. He was also set to be an ever-present in 1987/88 but was sent off at Manchester City four matches from the end of the season and missed the crucial last match through suspension – a 3-2 home defeat against Ipswich Town that cost them promotion to the old First Division. He returned for the two-legged play-off semi-final against Middlesbrough, which City lost 3-2 on aggregate after extra time and left the club to join Newcastle United for a £500,000 fee. He later played for Leeds United, Middlesbrough and Barnsley, where he became player manager. Hendrie made 173 league appearances, and 28 in the League and FA Cups, scoring a total of 55 goals.

Stuart McCall's commitment and consistency were legendary during his two spells as a City player and during his first spell he made 134 consecutive appearances, from halfway through the 1982/83 season to midway through the 1985/86 campaign, which meant that he was an ever-present in two successive seasons – 1983/84 and 1984/85.

HAT-TRICK HEROES

Eddie Carr, Jack Deacon and Frank O'Rourke boast the most hat-tricks by a Bradford City player. During a four-year career at the club between 1949 and 1953, Carr scored five hat-tricks, including a four-goal haul in a 9-0 win over Fleetwood in an FA Cup first-round tie at Valley Parade on Saturday 26th November 1949 only a month after joining the club from Newport County. Carr, a classic goal poacher, scored 56 league and cup goals in 99 appearances for City. His best season was his last at Valley Parade – 1952/53 – when he was leading scorer with 20 league goals, including eight in three matches over a five-day Easter programme with hat-tricks in both matches against Carlisle United. Carr played for Arsenal before World War II and guested for Bradford Park Avenue during the war. After leaving City he became a coach and manager with Darlington and also managed Tow Law Town. Jack Deakin Jack Deakin's Valley Parade career was brief, lasting just over two years, during which time he made 68 league and cup appearances, but what a superb goals-per-match ratio he enjoyed – 51 goals, including five hattricks – four three-goal tallies and one four-goal haul. Deakin, a miner from the village of Altofts in South Yorkshire, joined City from junior club Altofts WRC in October 1936, during City's last season in the old Second Division, but he struggled to gain a place in the first team, making only four appearances in his first season. However, following City's relegation to the old Third Division (North), he gained a regular place, scoring 20 league goals in 30 appearances and six in as many FA Cup games. He scored two league hat-tricks that season; in a 4-0 win against Carlisle and in a 3-2 victory against Rotherham – both at home – as well as his only four-goal haul in the 11-3 demolition of north-east non-league club Walker Celtic in an FA Cup first-round replay. Deakin didn't have a regular place in the side the following season, but he then played 26 consecutive matches and ended the campaign with a remarkable 23 goals in 28 league games, including hattricks in a 6-0 home win over York City, and a 4-0 win at Darlington.

HOTSHOT O'ROURKE

Frank O'Rourke joined City in unusual circumstances. The robust, bustling, hard shooting Scottish centre forward played for Airdrieonians in a friendly at Valley Parade in April 1907 and so impressed City officials that they roused him from his bed in a Leeds hotel that night to talk with the club.

O'Rourke, then 28, was an immediate success, scoring on his debut, and then four goals in five matches to the end of the season. O'Rourke was then at his peak and was top scorer in three of the next four campaigns. His best season was his first full campaign at Valley Parade when he scored 21 goals in 36 matches as City won promotion to the First Division as Second Division champions. His personal highlight was four goals in City's 7-1 thrashing of Gainsborough Trinity. He also scored a hat-trick in a 6-0 home win over Stoke City. Then, just as importantly, he played a key role in helping City stay in the top flight. He played in all 38 league matches, top scoring with 19 goals, including the priceless goal as they ensured their survival with a 1-0 win over Manchester City in front of a 30,000 crowd at Valley Parade. O'Rourke then helped City establish themselves in the top flight in 1909/10, scoring 20 goals, including three hat-tricks. He was leading scorer the following season with 13 goals in 32 matches as City achieved their highest-ever placing – fifth in the top division – before winning the FA Cup. He also played in all seven cup matches.

GOOD DON

Don Goodman scored a hat-trick in 14 minutes after coming on as substitute in an FA Cup first-round tie against north-east non-league club Tow Law Town at Valley Parade on November 17th 1984. City won 7-2 with Bobby Campbell (2), Stuart McCall and John Hendrie the other scorers. Goodman, who completed his apprenticeship as an electrician with Leeds City Council before signing as a professional with City, later played for West Bromwich Albion, Sunderland and Wolves. He now works as a commentator with Sky TV.

BIG TRANSFER SIGNINGS

Scottish international midfielder David Hopkin is City's most expensive player, but what a failed signing he proved to be. Hopkin joined City in a £2.5 million deal from Leeds United in July 2000 during what was dubbed 'the summer of madness'. That deal was part of an extraordinary spending spree after the club survived their first season in the Premier League. The former Chelsea and Crystal Palace player made a mere 11 league appearances, including three as substitute, and was transferred to Palace after less than a season at Valley Parade.

WASTE OF MONEY?

Other big money signings that summer included Chelsea's Romanian international midfielder Dan Petrescu for £1 million. Petrescu, who turned down Southampton for a better offer at Valley Parade, was not a success at City either. Petrescu, a favourite at Stamford Bridge, was not a success at City and, after making only 17 league appearances, he moved to Southampton before retiring from English football at the end of the season in 2002.

AN EYE-CATCHING SIGNING

The most eye-catching signing of the 'summer of madness' was Benito Carbone. The football world was staggered when chairman Geoffrey Richmond completed the audacious signing of the mercurial Italian forward on a four-year contract worth an astonishing £40,000 a week after night-time negotiations in Milan. Carbone was unveiled to City supporters at a noisy, public press conference at Valley Parade where journalists were often shouted down when they tackled Richmond with sceptical questions challenging the wisdom of the signing. It would be unfair to say that the skilful Italian was a failure at Valley Parade, but he wasn't a success either and after City were relegated the Bantams struggled to pay his wages and he spent loan spells at Middlesbrough and Derby County before the club were forced to come to a settlement on his lucrative contract as financial storm clouds began to gather. He made 42 league appearances, scoring ten goals for City, but, although the crowd enjoyed his silky skills, he wasn't the type of player the club needed as they battled in vain for Premier League survival.

ASHLEY WARD

Another £1 million-plus signing in the summer 2000 was striker Ashley Ward. He joined the club 24 hours before the new season began from Blackburn Rovers in a £1.5 million deal. His four-year contract was reported to be worth £18,000 per week. Ward's Valley Parade career was affected by injury and he didn't score as many goals as the club hoped – only 17 in 84 league appearances. Not surprisingly, City, who endured two administrations in three years, could not afford Ward's wages and he spent the final year of his contract at Sheffield United – his 11th club that also included Norwich City, Derby County and Barnsley. The club were forced to come to an agreement with Ward for the money they owed the player before they could come out of administration in 2004.

THREE MILLION-POUNDERS

City spent £4.5 million in achieving promotion to the Premier League in 1998/999, including three £1 million players, Lee Mills, Isaiah Rankin and Dean Windass. Mills was a great success and was top scorer with 23 goals while Windass also played a key goalscoring role in two spells at the club. However, striker Rankin failed to hold down a regular place after City had paid Arsenal a reported £1.3 million for him in August 1998. Rankin had not played any first-team games for Arsenal and his experience of league football was ten appearances on loan to Colchester United. He was edged out of City's promotion team by Lee Mills and Robbie Blake and made only 37 league appearances over two-and-a-half years, 22 of them as substitute, and scored a mere four goals. He was loaned to Bolton Wanderers and Birmingham City during his Valley Parade spell before he was transferred to Barnsley. He later played with Grimsby Town and Brentford.

DAVID WETHERALL

Once City had achieved promotion to the Premier League, manager Paul Jewell decided he needed to strengthen his defence with a player who had experience of playing at the top level. So he signed the Leeds United defender David Wetherall for a then club record £1.4 million. City have made few better signings in their modern history. Wetherall made more than 300 league and cup appearances in a nine-year playing career, including spells as captain and caretaker player-manager, and stayed on at Valley Parade after calling time on his playing career to become youth-team manager. Wetherall, who arrived at Valley Parade in June 1999, began his career with his hometown Sheffield Wednesday before moving to Leeds where he made 202 league appearances, scoring 12 goals over a seven-year spell.

And, Wetherall wrote his name into City's folklore at the end of his first season when he headed the winning goal against Liverpool that ensured the Bantams' Premier League survival after one year in the top flight. Wetherall had a long spell out of action the following season with a serious groin injury, but overcame that setback with characteristic fortitude. He was appointed captain in May 2002 when Stuart McCall left for Sheffield United and was soon involved in delicate negotiations regarding contracts after the club went into administration. A calm and wise figurehead, Wetherall played an influential role in keeping the players together through the administration crises of 2002 and 2004, setting an example by agreeing to defer the money owed to him through his contract.

He continued to stick with City through the difficult administration years and subsequent relegations in 2001, 2004 and 2007 before moving into full-time coaching. He was first given the opportunity to do some coaching after Colin Todd succeeded Bryan Robson as manager during the 2004 administration, and subsequent relegation, and he was placed in temporary charge when City sacked Todd in February 2007 – but he could not prevent City from being relegated. At the end of the season, the club appointed McCall as manager and he re-appointed Wetherall as captain for the new campaign. But it proved to be his last as a player as he pulled down the curtain on his playing career in May 2008. Wetherall stayed at Valley Parade for another three seasons as reserve team manager and youth team manager and was assistant manager to Peter Jackson for two months after he succeed Peter Taylor in March 2011. He left in the summer of 2011 to become head of youth development at the Football League.

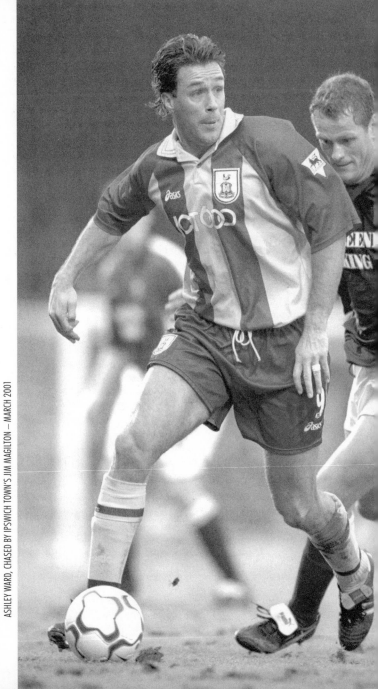

AN EARLY TRANSFER RECORD

City set a new transfer record in May 1921 when they signed Scottish leftback Billy Watson from Airdrieonians for £3,000. Watson made his debut in what proved to be City's last First Division season for 77 years and gave ten years of excellent service, making 347 league and FA Cup appearances – 330 of them in the league before losing his place and moving to Third Division (North) Walsall to finish his career. Watson twice suffered the heartache of relegation, but he also had the satisfaction of helping City back into the Second Division as Third Division (North) as champions in 1928/29.

AND ANOTHER...

Tommy Hoyland looked to be a great signing when he joined City from Sheffield United in a record £8,000 deal in October 1961. The then 29-year-old half-back had been an institution at his hometown club over a 12-year period, making 181 league appearances and scoring 18 goals. It was anticipated he would be a key player as manager Bob Brocklebank tried to build a team capable of gaining promotion back to the Third Division following their relegation the season before, but what a disappointment Hoyland turned out to be at Valley Parade. He made his debut in a 1-1 home draw against Barrow on Saturday 28th October 1961, but he turned out to be a peripheral figure as City made a determined, but unsuccessful, bid to finish in one of the four promotion places. He made only 27 league appearances over two seasons, scoring six goals, and was released at the end of the 1962/63 campaign when City had to seek re-election after finishing next to the bottom of the table. He never played league football again, deciding to concentrate on his shop business in Sheffield.

KEN LEEK

City broke their transfer record in October 1965 when they signed 30-yearold Welsh international centre forward Ken Leek from Northampton for £10,000 following an injection of cash by the new board headed by Stafford Heginbotham and David Ide. Leek, who won 17 Wales caps, also played at the top level for Leicester City and Birmingham City. Unfortunately for City, Leek wasn't the success the club hoped he would be. He couldn't save them from having to seek re-election in his first season although he finished as top scorer with 11 goals in 24 league appearances. He ended his Valley Parade career as a midfielder. He left City in June 1968 to join Rhyl Athletic as player-coach. He also played for another Welsh side, Tom Pentre, before retiring.

RECORD-BREAKING AFTERNOON

City set new transfer records twice in one afternoon – February 7, 1978 – when they first signed defender Mick Wood from Blackburn Rovers in a £15,000 deal, before signing Leeds United reserve striker David McNiven some two hours later for £25,000. Wood made 168 league and cup appearances over four years before ending his career at Halifax Town. McNiven scored 66 goals in 245 league and cup matches before moving to Blackpool in February 1983.

ANOTHER RECORD SIGNING!

Striker Mark Leonard became City's latest record signing when he joined the club in October 1986 for £40,000 from Stockport County, a couple of weeks after manager Trevor Cherry sold free-scoring Bobby Campbell to Wigan Athletic. Not surprisingly, the hardworking Leonard could not match Campbell's goalscoring record, but he made 157 league appearances, 37 of them as substitute, scoring 29 goals in a five-year spell at Valley Parade before City sold him to Rochdale in 1991. Leonard, who began his career as a junior with Everton, played for Tranmere and Crewe Alexandra before joining Stockport County. After leaving Rochdale in 1992, he played for Preston North End, Chester City and Wigan Athletic before ending his league career back at Rochdale, having scored 95 league goals in 498 appearances.

LEE SINNOTT

Lee Sinnott broke a new club record when he joined City in the 1987 close season in a £130,000 deal from Watford. The tall, pacy central defender was one of two key signings made that summer by manager Terry Dolan – goalkeeper Paul Tomlinson, a £47,000 signing from Sheffield United was the other. Sinnott had begun his career in his native Midlands with Walsall and made 40 appearances for the Saddlers before joining Watford, where he played in the 1984 FA Cup Final against Liverpool when he was still only 18. Sinnott, a former England youth international who played one game for the under-21s side, played 214 league matches and 32 cup games in three spells with City and was a key member of the side that was beaten in the Second Division play-off semi-finals in 1988. After four years at the club he transferred to Crystal Palace in the summer of 1991 for £350,000. He returned to Valley Parade two years later for £50,000 before being sold a year later to Huddersfield Town along with Lee Duxbury. He later played for Oldham Athletic before returning to Valley Parade for a brief loan spell at the end of the 1997/98 season under former teammate Paul Jewell. After his playing career was over Sinnott went into management and guided Farsley Celtic into Conference North before moving to Port Vale, and then back into non-league football with Bradford Park Avenue.

BRIAN MITCHELL

City broke the transfer record again later that season when new manager Terry Dolan, successor to Trevor Cherry, paid Aberdeen £70,000 for rightback Brian Mitchell. Mitchell, who had played European football for Aberdeen under Alex Ferguson before he left for Manchester United, was a classy footballer, who made 178 league appearances before moving to Bristol City and Hull City, where injury cut short his career.

ADDING SOME STEEL

As City survived two administration crises since the turn of the century, payment of transfer fees have been extremely rare. That makes the club's wheeling and dealing in six-figure deals in the late 1980s and early 1990s seem extraordinary in these prudent times. Manager Terry Dolan paid Portsmouth a club record £250,000 for their toughtackling midfielder Mick Kennedy in January 1988 to try to add some steel to the side in their pursuit of promotion. However, six weeks after Terry Yorath replaced Dolan just over a year later, he exchanged him for Leicester City striker Jimmy Quinn in a deal again valued at £250,000. Quinn lasted a mere nine months at Valley Parade until he was sold to West Ham for £320,000.

The sales of Stuart McCall to Everton for £850,000 and John Hendrie for £500,000 in the summer of 1988 sparked a flurry of transfer activity as manager Terry Dolan used the money to strengthen his squad. He paid Newcastle United £80,000 for midfield player Andy Thomas and the same amount to Wigan Athletic for striker Paul Jewell, he bought midfield player Ian Banks from Huddersfield Town for £180,000 before breaking the club's transfer record again by bringing back Peter Jackson from Newcastle for £290,000.

The day after Terry Dolan was sacked as manager at the end of January 1989, City sold striker Ian Ormondroyd to Aston Villa, then managed by future England boss Graham Taylor, for £650,000 and the appointment of Terry Yorath later that week sparked another spending spree. Yorath paid Newcastle United £150,000 for left back Brian Tinnion, £215,000 to Leeds United for Welsh international midfield player Mark Aizlewood, £135,000 to his old club Swansea for another Welsh international midfield player Alan Davies, £215,000 to Northampton for striker Tony Adcock and £200,000 to Glasgow Rangers for winger Ian McCall. A free kick and penalty specialist, Tinnion gave four years of good service, making 145 League appearances with 22 goals before moving to Bristol City where he played more than 400 matches before becoming player manager. The others stayed less than two years.

The Bantams broke their transfer record again in July 1994, when they agreed to pay £300,000 for 29-year-old striker John Taylor from Bristol Rovers – manager Lennie Lawrence's first big signing The clubs agreed to split the difference between the £500,000 that Rovers were asking and the £100,000 that City were offering. After scoring 11 goals in 36 League matches, Taylor was on the move again – this time to Luton Town.

He then had loan spells with Lincoln and his first club Colchester before rejoining another former club Cambridge United and then ending his career with Northampton.

RECORD DEAL FOR WATSON

Chris Kamara made three big signings during 1997. After being restricted in his signings policy in the first half of the 1996-7 as the club paid off the money owed on the new £4.5 million Midland Road stand, Kamara spent big in the calendar year 1997. First, he signed striker Gordon Watson from Southampton for new record £500,000 in the January, but three weeks later he lost the former Sheffield Wednesday and England under-21 player with a horrific double fracture of his right leg following a tackle by Huddersfield Town defender. Watson, who was out of action for more than 12 months, was later awarded £900,000 in compensation after the club and player began legal proceedings against Huddersfield and their player. Watson made a comeback with City, but he made only 21 League appearances in total, 13 of them as substitute and scored eight goals in two years at Valley Parade. He later moved to Bournemouth before winding up his career with Hartlepool.

Kamara also paid Middlesbrough £500,000 the following season for former Manchester United goalkeeper Gary Walsh and he made 132 league appearances in a five year spell at Valley Parade that included promotion to the Premier League two seasons in the top flight. However, later that month – November 1997 – he broke the club record by signing Scottish international striker John McGinlay from Bolton in a bid to solve City's goalscoring problems – the fee £625,000. McGinlay had scored 118 goals in 245 appearances, but he was dogged by injury in his 12 months at Valley Parade and the following season, with Paul Jewell having succeeded Kamara, the club settled the remaining 21 months of his contract. McGinlay had scored a mere three goals in 17 League appearances. The most eye catching signing of Kamara's spell as manager was the former England winger Chris Waddle.

He joined the club in October 1996 after playing on a short term contract with Falkirk and delighted the City fans with his inventive skills during his five months at the club before moving to Sunderland. The highlight was undoubtedly his 40 yard lob that helped City to beat Everton at Goodison Park in the FA Cup. Waddle, now a BBC Five Liver soccer pundit, enjoyed an illustrious career, winning 62 England caps and making 465 League appearances, 25 of them with City and scoring 96 goals. Born in the North East, he began his career with Newcastle and continued with Spurs and Sheffield Wednesday. He enjoyed a spell in France with Marseille and had a season as player manager with Burnley before ending his career with Torquay.

BARGAIN BUYS

City's most famous player must also their biggest bargain even set against transfer values of 1909. Dickie Bond was one of the best – if not the best – outside rights in the early 1900s, but when the 26-year-old joined City from Preston North End in May 1909 his fitness was in doubt because of a knee injury. The club doctor examined Bond's knee and, despite his doubts he advised the club to take a chance and Bond joined City for a bargain fee of £950. Dodgy knee or not, Bond played in 332 League FA Cup matches and scored 73 goals in a 13-year career at Valley Parade, interrupted by World War I. All his 301 League appearances were made in the top division. Even after he left City following their relegation from the First Division in 1922, he still played one more season at Blackburn Rovers before ending his career at non-League Lancaster City. The move to City also revived his international career and he regained his place in the England team, playing in all three home internationals in the 1910-11 season. Bond missed City's only appearance in the FA Cup final – in 1911 – because he was suspended for using improper language with the crowd during a match at Arsenal. He joined the Bradford Pals and served as a machine gunner at the Battle of the Somme in 1916 and was taken prisoner. He spent two years as a prisoner of war and the Germans were so proud of their famous captive that they put up a notice saying 'We captured Dickie Bond.'

Dickie Bond's regular inside forward partner Oscar Fox was also a bargain buy, when City signed him from non-League Castleford Town in November 1910. The fee was £100. It might sound like petty cash now, but, apparently, Castleford were delighted to accept and it was regarded as a 'rattling good fee' in those days according to their manager Leslie Knighton, who later managed Arsenal, Chelsea and Huddersfield Town among others. Fox made 175 League and FA Cup appearances in an 11-year career at Valley Parade, scoring 58 goals.

City's 1984-5 Third Division championship team included three outstanding free transfer signings. Right back Greg Abbott had joined them from Coventry two years earlier and he was joined in the summer of 1984 by his former Coventry team-mate winger John Hendrie and defender Dave Evans from Halifax Town. What outstanding service they gave the club. Not only did they help City win promotion to the old Second Division, but gave outstanding service after that. Abbott played for the club for nine years, making 321 League and cup appearances, scoring 47 goals before continuing his career with Halifax Town, Guiseley and Hull City. Evans played in 260 League and cup games over seven years before returning to Halifax while Hendrie made 201 League and cup appearances before leaving Valley Parade for Newcastle in 1988 in a £500,000 deal. He later played for Leeds United, Middlesbrough and Barnsley where he was also manager for a season.

Ian Ormondroyd was playing non-League football with Bradford club Thackley when City invited him to join them and, after scoring 20 goals in 87 League appearances over the next two and a half years they received £650,000 for him from Aston Villa, and then managed by future England manager Graham Taylor. The 6ft 4ins striker went on to play for Derby County and Leicester City before returning to Valley Parade in the summer of 1995 an stayed for two more years before moving to Oldham and Hull – two clubs where he had enjoyed loan spells. He is now the club's Community Foundation Officer. One of City's free transfer signings of modern times was left back, current assistant manager Wayne Jacobs, who joined them on a free transfer from Rotherham United in the summer of 1994 and went to make well over 300 League and cup appearances before returning as assistant manager.

JAMES HANSON – WHAT A BARGAIN!

Even in these days of huge transfer fees and astronomical wages in the Premier League, clubs in the lower divisions are increasingly shopping in the non-leagues for players and former City manager Stuart McCall did that successfully in the 2009 season, signing striker James Hanson from Unibond Premier League neighbours Guiseley. Hanson, who had been leading scorer at Guiseley in the previous two seasons, scoring 46 goals in 67 appearances in total, was an obvious target for his local Football League club. He signed his first professional contract with City in July 2009, but the clubs could not agree on a fee and so it was left to a tribunal to set a £7,500 fee with a sell-on clause and an agreement for a friendly between City and Guiseley. Hanson worked in a local Co-operative store and worked his notice while taking part in pre-season training at Valley Parade. He made an inauspicious debut as City crashed to a 5-0 defeat at Notts County on the opening day of the season, but things improved after that and he scored his first goal in an extraordinary 5-4 win at Cheltenham a fortnight later. Hanson was an instant success, winning the club's player of the year award and was rewarded with an improved four-year contract. He scored 14 goals in 2011-12, his highest tally as a full-time professional in manager Phil Parkinson's first season with the club. The striker was one of the heroes of City's momentous 2012-13 season, forming a potent partnership with Nahki Wells and scoring vital goals – 14 in all – as the Bantams twice went to Wembley – for the Capital One League Cup Final and the League Two play-off final.

They captured the national headlines as they reached the League Cup Final – an amazing achievement for a League Two club. City beat three Premier League clubs, Wigan Athletic, Arsenal and Aston Villa, on the way to Wembley where they were outplayed by Swansea in a 5-0 defeat and it was Hanson, who scored the vital goal in the semi-final, second leg at Villa Park that helped the Bantams to achieve a 4-3 aggregate win after they had beaten Villa 3-1 in the first leg at Valley Parade. His performance and the goal at Villa Park earned him the man of the match award. Hanson also scored another crucial goal in the second leg of the League Two play-off semi-final against Burton Albion to help City overcome a 3-2 deficit from the home leg to win the game 3-1 and the tie 5-4 on aggregate. And, so City returned to Wembley three months after their League Cup Final defeat and this time there was a happy ending as Hanson scored one of the goals in their comfortable 3-0 win over Northampton in the play-off final to achieve promotion. Promotion to League One provided another challenge for Hanson, but he proved to be equal to the task, scoring 12 goals, all in the League as he passed the 50-League goal mark during the season and earned a new contract, which will keep him at the club until the end of the 2016-17 season. A successful start to the 2014-15 season took him into the club's top ten all-time scorers' list and once again he hit the national headlines by scoring a late winning goal as City beat West Yorkshire rivals Leeds United 2-1 in the League Cup second round at Valley Parade.

We have become used to Chelsea's big spending under Roman A in recent years, but, apparently, they were also big spenders 100 years ago. Then, Chelsea spent £3,575 on five players in six days, the most expensive of whom was City centre forward Bob Whittingham. City received £1,300 for 22-year-old Whittingham, who had scored 31 goals in 45 League appearances since joining the Bantams from Blackpool 12 months earlier.

BOB WHITTINGHAM

Whittingham was one of City's major signings as they battled for First Division survival after winning the Second Division championship the season before and he scored ten ten goals in the last 17 matches to help the club avoid relegation. He then scored 21 goals in 28 League matches the following season before being sold to Chelsea after scoring a hat-trick against the Blues in City's 4-1 win at Valley Parade on the first Saturday

in April. Clearly, they were impressed by his efforts.

City were forced to sell one of their best ever players Sam Barkas to Manchester City in April 1934, receiving a club record £5,000 fee. As often was the case, City were struggling financially and the story at the time was that the money they received for the future England left back was needed to pay the summer wages. Barkas, one of five brothers, who played professional football, joined City in August 1927 from Middle Dock, a Tyneside junior team. Writing 14 years after his transfer to Manchester City, Barkas said: "My unhappiest moment in Bradford came when I left after seven delightful seasons. But for my old club being in financial straights I would have stayed at Valley Parade, my first love. The homely feeling at Valley Parade would have made anybody down in the mouth at the thought of leaving, but the club had to keep the flag flying and if the money they received for my transfer helped me to do that I was happy in my unhappiness."

BIG PROFIT ON SCHWARZER

City made a large profit on Australian born goalkeeper Mark Schwarzer. Manager Chris Kamara signed Schwarzer from German League club Kaiserslautern in October 1996 for a reported £325,000, but, four months and a mere 16 matches later, Schwarzer was on his way to Premier League Middlesbrough, fulfilling his ambition to play at the top level in the English game, preferring them to Everton, who were also keen to sign him. City's consolation was a reported £1.5 million. Schwarzer enjoyed a successful 11 years at Middlesbrough before joining Fulham and helping them to reach the Europa Cup final against Athletico Madrid at Hamburg in May 2010.

DEREK HAWKSWORTH

One of Bradford's best players in the early post war period was winger Derek Hawksworth, who joined City in 1948 after playing with Bradford Park Avenue and Huddersfield Town as an amateur. After a successful two years at Valley Parade, he was transferred to Sheffield United for a £12,500 fee and played 255 League matches in a seven year spell for the Blades, scoring 88 goals and winning an England B against France in 1952. He later played for Huddersfield Town and Lincoln City before ending his League career back at Valley Parade.

PETER JACKSON

Defender Peter Jackson, who captained City to the Third Division championship in 1984-5, left the club 18 months later to join First Division club Newcastle United in a £250,000 deal – in October 1986. Jackson enjoyed two seasons in the top flight with Newcastle, winning the club's Player of he Year award and making 60 League appearances and scoring three goals before he made a surprise return to Valley Parade in September 1988 in a reported £290,000 deal. He made another 58 League appearances for the club, but the move was not a success as Jackson admitted. "It never worked out for me," he said. "My biggest regret is that I came back and let so many people down." That was a pity for Jackson will always have a special place in the club's history. Only six players in the 107-year history of the club have played in more League matches – he made 336 League appearances as a committed central defender in his two spells at Valley Parade. The club's youngest ever captain – he was made skipper at 19 – and, after leading a predominantly young side to the Third Division title, he won the admiration of all for the way he conducted himself as skipper during the trauma and aftermath of the Valley Parade fire tragedy. Born in Bradford, but brought up in Keighley, he joined Burnley as a schoolboy, but he was released and joined City as a 16-year-old in 1977 and became a full-time professional in April 1979. The highlight of his City career was undoubtedly captaining the Third Division Championship winning team, but after receiving the trophy and leading the players on a lap honour triumph turned to tragedy as fire engulfed the main stand at Valley Parade, 56 lost their lives and hundreds more were injured.

After leaving City for the second time, Jackson moved to Huddersfield Town on a free transfer in September 1990 – a move that proved to be successfully as he made 155 League appearances in four seasons before ending his career with Chester, where he played a further 100 League appearances before retiring. He later managed Huddersfield twice and was also manager of Lincoln City. He also had the chance to return to Valley Parade as manager when Jim Jefferies left the club in December 2001, but turned down chairman Geoffrey Richmond's offer.

QUINN JOINS HAMMERS

The sale of Northern Ireland striker Jimmy Quinn to West Ham United for £320,000 in December 1989 might have cost City their Second Division status. Quinn had joined City from Leicester in a straight swap for midfield player Mick Kennedy in the March soon after Terry Yorath arrived as manager and did well until the end of the season. He didn't do nearly as well the following season, but he had the class and potential to recover his form and, although Yorath was promised he could use the money to strengthen the team he never replaced him. City continued to struggle for goals, Yorath lost his job and the team were relegated.

Defender Dean Richards was one of the best young players City have produced, but sadly his career was cut short by illness in 2003 when he was only 29. Bradford born Richards, who joined City as a youth trainee, signed as a full-time professional in 1992 and made his debut at 17, scoring in a 3-1 win at Bournemouth. He immediately impressed as a polished defender, who liked to play the ball out of defence and was clearly destined for higher-grade football. So, it was no surprise when he left City in March 1995 in one of chairman Geoffrey Richmond's multi-clause deals. It was expected that Richards, who made 97 League and cup appearances for City, would move into the Premier League, but the top clubs were clearly not convinced about his ability. So, it was a second tier club Wolverhampton Wanderers, who took the plunge, signing him first on loan and then in a transfer deal that was initially valued at £1.3 million, but rose to £1.8 million when various clauses took effect.

Richards made 122 League appearances in four years at Wolves, gained four England under-21 caps and he was still at Molineux in May 1999 when City won a thrilling last match to seal their automatic promotion to the Premier League. When his four-year contract expired at Wolves there was speculation that Richards would return to Valley Parade and play Premier League football with his home town club. However, manager Paul Jewell signed David Wetherall as his new central defender that summer and Richards got his wish to play in the top flight when he joined Southampton on a free transfer. He spent just over two years at Southampton, making 67 League appearances, first under David Jones and then under former England manager Glen Hoddle. Then, when Hoddle moved to Tottenham Hotspur he signed Richards in October 2001 for £8 million. Richards, who made 73 League appearances for Spurs, played his last match in May 2003 when he was forced to announce his retirement after medical experts warned that his dizzy spells could lead to a brain haemorrhage if he continued to play. After his career was over he was involved with a company in Spain and worked as a coach at City's Centre of Excellence. Sadly, he died in 2011 aged 36.

Bradford born midfield player Des Hamilton will be mainly remembered as the scorer of the first goal in City's 2-0 win over Notts County in the Third Division play-off final at Wembley in May 1996. His career looked set to take off when Kenny Dalglish signed him for Newcastle United ten months later in £1.5 million deal, but it never happened. Soon after his move, Hamilton was selected for England under-21s. City manager Chris Kamara had frequently put his forward to the selectors, but it was only when he moved to the Premier League that he was chosen. Unfortunately, Hamilton was never able to win a regular first team place at Newcastle and, in four years at St James' Park, Hamilton spent most of his time in the reserves, making just 12 League appearances, five of them as substitute. He went on loan to four clubs – Sheffield United, Huddersfield Town, Norwich City and Tranmere Rovers before he secured another permanent move to Cardiff City and from there to Grimsby Town. In recent years he has been playing local football back in Bradford. By far

the most successful period of his career was as a promising teenager at Valley Parade. He was developed through the club's youth scheme and played in City's team that reached FA Cup semi-final against Arsenal in 1994 and he went on to make 88 League appearances, 21 of them from the substitutes' bench and scoring five goals for his home town club.

Another player from that FA Youth Cup team was striker Graeme Tomlinson, who became a regular as an 18-year-old in the first team in the second half of the 1993-4 season, scoring six goals in 17 League matches, five of them as substitute. City offered him a contract for the following season, hoping to build on his undoubted potential. However, Manchester United had also taken a fancy to the Keighley based youngster and, tempted by a move to Old Trafford, he turned down City's offer and signed a four-year contract with United. City received a fee of £100,000 and chairman Geoffrey Richmond negotiated several clauses for extra payments based on appearances, international honours and future sales. Sadly for the club and the player, none of them came to fruition. For, Tomlinson did not make a single first team appearance at Old Trafford although he went on loan to Luton, Bournemouth and Millwall. He had the misfortune to break a leg during his spell at Luton and was eventually transferred to Macclesfield and then Exeter before drifting out League football in 2001, when he was only 26. In all, he made 81 full League appearances and as many as 55 substitute appearances, scoring 20 goals.

IRISH HONOURS

Defender Andy O'Brien was another City youngster who moved to Newcastle United in a £1.5 million deal, but, unlike Des Hamilton, O'Brien is enjoying a successful career in the Premier League. The Harrogate born player had a trial at Leeds United before joining City as a 15-year-old and made his League debut at Queens Park Rangers in October 1996 aged 17. O'Brien went on to gain a regular place in the team and helped them to win promotion to the Premier League in 1998-9 and helped them to stay there with the 1-0 win in that memorable final match of the season against Liverpool.

After making 146 League and cup appearances over four seasons, he was transferred to Newcastle just before transfer deadline in 2001 – towards the end of City's second season in the Premier League with the Bantams heading towards relegation. O'Brien played four seasons at Newcastle before he was on the move again, this time to Portsmouth where he stayed for two years before joining Bolton in 2007. O'Brien has also enjoyed a successful international career with the Republic of Ireland for whom he qualifies through his grandparents, his father's parents, who were born in County Limerick. He did play for England youth teams and England under-21s, but then switched to the Republic for his senior international football.

BIG TWO MOVE ON

The two biggest sales in the 1980s came within a couple of weeks of each other. When City failed to gain promotion to the old First Division in 1987-8 – they lost to Middlesbrough in the play-off semi-final – it was inevitable that the Bantams would lose their two best players. So, within a month of that disappointing night at Middlesbrough, Stuart McCall was on his way to Everton in an £850,000 deal while Hendrie joined Newcastle for £500,000.

As new manager John Docherty was trying to build a team capable of winning promotion back to the Second Division in the summer of 1990, he received a call from a 19-year-old player, who had just been released by his former club Millwall. Phil Babb asked his mentor what he should do and, without hesitation, Docherty told him to catch the next train to Bradford. It was the start of a successful career that was to take him from City to Coventry, Liverpool, Sporting Lisbon and Sunderland. Babb initially played in the centre of defence, but Docherty moved him to centre forward during his first season and he scored some useful goals. Babb was on the move after two seasons with City during which he played 80 League matches, scoring 14 goals when the club accepted a £300,000 offer from Coventry City and two years later Babb got an even bigger move – £2.7 million to Liverpool.

He played four years at Anfield, making 128 League appearances as a defender before moving to Sporting Lisbon for four years and then back to England to finish his career with Sunderland. Although in the London borough of Lambeth, Babb qualified to play for the Republic of Ireland and won 35 full caps with the Irish side. Although City were delighted with the £300,000 fee they received from Coventry, when Babb later moved to Liverpool for nine times that amount the then chairman Geoffrey Richmond was disgusted that his predecessors had not added some of his trademark clauses so that the club would benefit from future sales.

FIRST PLAYER BOSS

Player managers became popular after the Second World War as top class players decided to continue their playing careers lower down the league while enjoying their first taste of management. City's first player manager was Jack Milburn, who arrived at Valley Parade as a coach in October 1946 when former England and Derby County defender Jack Barker was manager. He succeeded Barker four months later and was manager for 18 months before resigning when David Steele took over in July 1948. He helped Steele with coaching before leaving the club.

Welsh international half back Ivor Powell became City's second player manager after the club parted company with David Steele in the summer of 1952, but, although he produced some fine performances on the field, his two and half years in charge was not successful. Powell, who was almost 36 when he arrived at Valley Parade, played a dominate role in midfield, showing City supporters what an outstanding player he must have been at the height of his career at Queens Park Rangers and Aston Villa. After finishing a disappointing 16th in his first season, City raised hopes of promotion in his second full season with a record-breaking run of nine successive wins in the second half of the campaign. However, once that run ended City failed to win a single one of their last ten matches and finished fifth. There was a promising start to the following campaign with six wins in the first ten matches.

Unfortunately, Powell was carried off with a knee ligament trouble in a home match against Wrexham in mid-September and, despite numerous attempts at a comeback, he never played again. Without Powell's leadership on the field, the side slumped in form and it was no surprise when he left the club the following February. Powell, who had been player manager of Port Vale, became trainer coach at Leeds United and managed Carlisle United and Bath City. He was still coaching at Bath University in his 90s and was inducted to the Welsh Sports Hall of Fame in 2004. He officially retired as a coach in 2010.

HARRIS TO THE RESCUE

City were at a low ebb late in the 1964-5 season when the club turned to Middlesbrough's former Welsh international half back Bill Harris to be their player manager. Swansea born Harris got his break in League football in 1950 when Hull City paid Llanelli £2,000 for his services. He made 131 appearances for Hull in the old Second Division before joining Middlesbrough for £15,000. He became a regular player at Middlesbrough, missing only ten League matches in his first five seasons with 64 goals – a good record for what we would call a midfield player nowadays. His best season was in 1961-2 when he was Boro's second highest scorer with 14 goals. Harris also gained six Welsh caps while he was at Boro, but, after making 360 League appearances and scoring 69 goals, he accepted City's offer to become player manager at Valley Parade. City were in danger of having to seek re-election when arrived six weeks before the end of the 1964-5 season, but he managed to steer them to safety, but things went downhill after that. He was plagued by injury the following season as City made a bad start and, although he was given money to spend on new players when a new board led by Stafford Heginbotham took over in October 1965 – Ken Leek was his star signing – he left the club part way through the campaign. Harris made six League appearances at t the end of his first season, but only three the following campaign due to injury.

Two England international defenders, Roy McFarland and Trevor Cherry led the club to promotion in the 1980s. McFarland, who won 28 caps, joined City from Derby County in May 1981 and proved to be an inspirational leaders as the Bantams won promotion from the Fourth Division in his only full season, finishing second behind Sheffield United. Although he didn't play in every match, McFarland, regarded as one of England classiest, ball playing centre halves since the war, made a key contribution on as well as off the field, giving ample evidence of his class during his 30 League appearances that season with his strong tackling, positional sense and ball distribution. However, he shocked the club when he walked out the following November with assistant Mick Jones to take charge at his old club Derby, the sudden departure coming on a November Sunday afternoon 24 hours after City had beaten Port Vale away in an FA Cup first round tie. Two days later they were installed as part of a new look management team at Derby as the club tried to re-create the great days under Brian Clough. Peter Taylor, Brian Clough's right hand man in Derby's great days of a decade earlier, was appointed general manager with McFarland as team manager assisted by Jones.

The move turned out to be a failure. Peter Taylor left the club, leaving McFarland with nine games to save Derby from relegation. He couldn't do it, but he stayed on to help former chief scout to lead Derby back up. McFarland continued his managerial career at Bolton where he was joint manager with future City manager Colin Todd and later managed Cambridge United and Torquay United before becoming manager at Chesterfield in 2003. However, with relegation looming, he was sacked in March 2007. He also had a spell as caretaker manager at Burton Albion towards the end of the 2008-09 season after Nigel Clough left to become Derby manager. Burton were top of the Conference and he helped them to win promotion to the Football League before leaving the club in the summer of 2009. McFarland made 46 League and cup appearances with City and 577 senior appearances in total, including 434 League matches for Derby, whom he joined from Tranmere Rovers in August 1967, one of Brian Clough's first signings. He also turned out to be one of his best signings and he was a key part of the team that won the Second Division championship in his first season, two League championships and the European Cup semi-finals.

Trevor Cherry was installed as McFarland's a month after his fellow England international left Valley Parade and, after coping with City's financial crisis the following summer, he led City to promotion as Third Division champions in his third season - 1984-5 - a predominantly, young, ambitious team. It was the first time for 48 years that City had managed to escape from the bottom two divisions. Tragically, the season ended with the Valley Parade fire disaster, but Cherry overcame the handicap of City having to play all their 'home' matches away from Valley Parade to guide the team into a midtable position in the old Second Division. Unfortunately, for him, he was sacked the following January just a monthly after the club to their re-built home ground, the victim of a run of poor results. Nonetheless, he is regarded highly by City supporters for his achievements and for the team he built with little money to spend, the players he signed, notably John Hendrie, Dave Evans, Greg Abbott, Chris With and Martin Singleton and the way the club's own young players like Stuart McCall, Peter Jackson and Mark Ellis developed under his guidance and that of coach, his former Elland Road team-mate Terry Yorath Cherry lost right hand man Yorath during the 1986 close season.

He left to become manager of Swansea City and was succeeded by youth team coach Terry Dolan, who then replaced Cherry when was surprisingly sacked seven months later. That proved to be the end of Cherry's football career that began with his home-town club Huddersfield Town, whom he captained to the Second Division title in 1970. He moved to Leeds when Town were relegated two years later and won a League Championship medal and appeared in FA Cup and European finals during ten years at Elland Road. Cherry made 102 League appearances for City and would have made more but for a knee injury in the home match against title rivals Millwall midway through the Third Division championship season. He never fully recovered from that setback and, although he played five more matches later that season, he retired as a player at the end of championship campaign. Cherry made 679 League appearances for three West Yorkshire clubs – Huddersfield, Leeds and City and 27 England caps.

Frank Stapleton was on a short term playing agreement with neighbours Huddersfield Town, helping his friend Eoin Hand when City chairman David Simpson approached him to succeed John Docherty as manager and he became player-boss in December 1992. The Republic of Ireland international centre forward had enjoyed an illustrious playing career with Arsenal and Manchester United, but failed to bring about an up turn in City's fortunes during his two and a half years at Valley Parade and they were still stuck in the third tier of English football when new chairman Geoffrey Richmond called time on his spell as manager a week before the end of the 1993-4 season. Born in Dublin, Stapleton began his career with Arsenal, where he played 225 League matches, scoring 75 goals before moving to Manchester United, where he enjoyed similar success, scoring 60 League goals in 223 appearances. After leaving Old Trafford, he continued his career with in Holland Ajax, at Blackburn Rovers and Le Havre in France before joining Huddersfield.

HONOURS ALL WAY FOR O'ROURKE

Peter O'Rourke was a player when he was appointed City's second manager in 1905 and he turned out to be the most successful manager in the club's history. He led them to the Second Division championship in 1908, FA Cup victory and their highest ever placing – fifth in the top division – in season 1910-11 and kept them in the top division before leaving the club in 1921, a year before they were relegated from the top flight. Then, in 1928, City called him back after they had been relegated from the Second Division and he led them to the Third Division North championship in 1928-9 before leaving the club for the last time in 1930 after they had survived their first season back in Division Two. O'Rourke was one of the first players to sign for City when the club was formed in 1903 and was their regular centre half in his first season. He was still a player and captain when he succeeded Robert Campbell as manager in November 1905 and gave up his playing career a month later to concentrate on management. What an inspired appointment! O'Rourke also managed Bradford Park Avenue, Pontypridd, Dundee Hibernians, Walsall and Llanelli.

O'Rourke's successor as manager was David Menzies, who had been a reserve player at Valley Parade when the club was formed in 1903 and was assistant trainer up to the outbreak of World War I. He later became trainer and then manager at Hull City before returning to Valley Parade with the daunting task of taking from O'Rourke with the immediate problem of keeping City in the First Division. Despite spending heavily on new players, City were relegated the following season after losing their last five matches and they never looked like regaining their First Division status during the next four years of Menzies' management. He resigned in June 1926 after another unsuccessful season and went on to take charge of Doncaster Rovers, leading them to the Third Division North championship before returning to Hull.

When Trevor Cherry was sacked in January 1987, City turned to first team coach Terry Dolan. Bradford born Dolan, who played briefly as an amateur for City, began his League career with Bradford Park Avenue for whom he played 48 League matches in their two seasons as a League club before moving to Huddersfield Town in 1971. He made 162 League appearances over a five-year spell with Huddersfield before joining City in August 1976 for a £10,000 fee. He played 217 League cup games for City as a midfield player, scoring 49 goals before he was released on a free transfer at the end of the 1980-1 season. He ended his playing career with Rochdale before moving into coaching. He was resident coach at Bradford Council's Centre of Excellence and coached at Harrogate Town before returning to Valley Parade as youth team coach in January 1985. He was then promoted to first team coach when Terry Yorath left to become manager of Swansea in the summer of 1986 before succeeding Trevor Cherry as manager in January 1987. Dolan beat off some big names to take the manager's job on a permanent basis, including Martin O'Neill and won over the sceptics among the City fans over in his first home match as the Bantams beat Oldham Athletic 5-1 in an FA Cup third round replay. Dolan enjoyed two successful years at Valley Parade, first saving them from relegation after City lost only one and winning eight of their last ten matches in 1986-7 before coming agonisingly close to promotion in the following season.

City were in an automatic promotion position going into the last week of the campaign, but lost their last two matches and had to settle for a place in the play-offs. They lost to Middlesbrough 3-2 in the two legged play-off semi-final and the chance of First Division football was lost. He lost his two best players, Stuart McCall and John Hendrie after failing to gain promotion and, unfortunately, his new signings did not come up to expectations and the following January, City decided to sack him after being knocked out of the FA and League Cups in the space of a fortnight. However, Dolan was soon back in the game and he went on to have a successful managerial career at Rochdale, Hull City and York City.

INTO TOP FLIGHT WITH JEWELL

Apart from Peter O'Rourke, the most successful ex-player to take over as manager at Valley Parade was Paul Jewell. The striker, who joined City for £80,000 in the summer of 1988, played 298 League and cup appearances, scoring 75 goals in an eight year spell before moving into coaching under Chris Kamara and then succeeding him as manager in January 1998. The appointment of Jewell as Kamara's successor was a surprise. As usual on these occasions, many supporters were calling for a so-called big name manager, but Jewell was given the job until the end of the season and, although, it was by no means a successful period in terms of results, chairman decided to appoint Jewell on a permanent basis and it turned out to be an inspired decision. Sensing that the division was not all that strong, Richmond and fellow directors, David and Julian Rhodes decided to go all out for promotion with some significant team strengthening, notably the return of Stuart McCall from Glasgow Rangers and centre forward Lee Mills from Port Vale. Jewell was manager for a mere two seasons, but they turned out to be the most successful in modern times. In his first full season he led the club to automatic promotion to the Premier League and, then, against all odds and the opinions of the pundits, he managed to keep City up thanks to a memorable 1-0 win over Liverpool in the last match of the season.

Unfortunately, for City supporters he left in the summer of 2000 following disagreements with chairman Geoffrey Richmond and the club went downhill after that, suffering three relegations in six years. He later managed Sheffield Wednesday before leading Wigan Athletic into the Premier League and keeping them there. After leaving Wigan, he took over at Derby County and resigned midway through the following campaign after failing to keep them in the Premier League.

TERRY YORATH

Terry Yorath had three management and coaching spells at Valley Parade. The former Welsh international midfield player, who began his career with Leeds United and later played for Tottenham Hotspur and Coventry City, joined his former Elland Road team-mate Trevor Cherry at City in December 1982 as player coach and proved to be an inspirational coach as he helped Cherry to develop the Bantams' Third Division Championship team in 1984-5. He left in the summer of 1986 to become manager of Swansea City, but returned in February 1989 to succeed Terry Dolan. Unfortunately, his spell as manager was not success despite considerable investment in the team and he lost his job 13 months later with City in danger of relegation from the old Second Division. He returned to Swansea for a second spell as manager and managed in Lebanon before teaming up with Peter Jackson after the former City captain was appointed manager of Huddersfield Town. After they both lost their jobs, he returned to Valley Parade for a third time when the then City manager Paul Jewell offered him the job as coach, but he left soon after Jewell quit City in June 2000 and joined him at Sheffield Wednesday before teaming up for a second time with Jackson at Huddersfield. They guided Town to promotion from the fourth tier – now League Two – through the 2004 play-offs, but when they were sacked for a second time he drifted out of the game.

STUART MCCALL

Stuart McCall is the most popular City player of modern times, but he had less success as a manager. After he left City for a second time as a player in May 2002, most supporters always longed for the day when he would come back as manager.

So, he received a hero's welcome when returned to at Valley Parade in 2007 after a spell as No 2 at Sheffield United following City's relegation to League Two, the fourth tier of English football. Unfortunately, he failed to lead his side to the play-offs in his first two seasons and resigned in February 2010 with City anchored in midtable.

After a nine months out of the game, McCall returned to football management with Scottish Premier League club Motherwell as successor to former Scotland boss Craig Brown and he has enjoyed a successful era at the Lanarkshire club. He led Motherwell to the semi-finals of both

Scottish Cup competitions in his first season and, although they were beaten in the League Cup, they won the Scottish Cup by beating St Johnstone 3-0 in the final. The following season he led them to a third place finish and qualification for the Champions League for the first time in their history and the season after that - 2012-13 - they finished third. The excellent reputation he enjoys in Scottish football was recognised In January 2013, when he was invited to join the backroom staff of Scotland manager Gordon Strachan.

BARKER'S BRIEF STAY

Famous players don't always make good managers. One good example is former England defender Jack Barker, who was City's first post war manager in 1946. Barker made 327 League appearances in a top class Derby team between the wars after joining them from Midland League club Denaby United in 1928 and won 11 England caps. He was appointed City manager after serving in the Army Physical Training Corps and made a promising start, leading them into fifth place in the Third Division North, but resigned after eight months in charge. After leaving Valley Parade, he had brief spells as manager of Irish club Dundalk and as trainer coach at Oldham Athletic before returning to League management with Derby in November 1953, replacing Stuart McMillan, son of Johnny McMillan, City's first captain. Unfortunately, with most of their internationals gone, he couldn't stop their slide and in 1955 Derby were relegated to the Third Division North for the first time in their history. Barker, who had earlier worked for Rolls Royce in Derby, went back to work in Derby, this time as a fitter's mate at a railway and carriage works.

Another famous player, who didn't enjoy much success at Valley Parade, was David Steele, who managed the club for four years between 1948 and 1952. A Scot, Steele was born in Lanarkshire and played football part-time with Armadale and St Mirren while he worked as a miner before World War I. After the war, he played with Scottish junior club Douglas Water Thistle before moving to England to play with Bristol Rovers, then in Southern League. He continued to play with Rovers when they became members of the newly formed Third Division in 1920. Then, he got his big move to Huddersfield Town in 1922.

Town, then managed by the famous Herbert Chapman, who later enjoyed success with Arsenal, gained international recognition with Scotland during his seven year spell at Huddersfield. As a member of the famous Steele-Wilson-Watson half back line, he helped Huddersfield to a hat-trick of League championships in the 1920s, two successive runners-up places and an FA Cup final appearance. He joined Preston on a free transfer in May 1929 and retired the following year. He worked as a coach

at Bury and Sheffield before being appointed manager of Bradford Park Avenue – then in the Second Division – in 1936. He continued managing Park Avenue after war broke out and played as an emergency centre forward and scored against Sheffield Wednesday in 1942. He resigned to join his old club Huddersfield as manager the following year, but when Town finished one place above the relegation positions although they were eight points above Brentford, he resigned. He was working on the family's fruit farm when City persuaded to return to football management, but City had to apply for re-election for the first time in their history in his first season – 1948-9 – and all he had show for his work at Valley Parade was a 3-2 victory in the West Riding Cup final against Leeds United in May 1950.

When City engaged Peter Jackson in March 1955, they not only gained a new manager, but two players well for, 18-year-old twins, David and Peter Jackson came with him to Bradford from his previous club Wrexham. David, a tall, skilful inside forward played 278 League and cup matches, scoring 68 goals while Peter, a hard working, tough tackling half back made 217 League and cup appearances, scoring 15 goals over the six year period their father was manager. They stayed together after being released by City in 1961 and played together at Tranmere Rovers for two years before David left to join Halifax Town while Peter stayed at Tranmere for an extra two years. They also played together in non-League football at Frickley Colliery, Altrincham and Hyde United. Jackson did so well in his first year at Valley Parade that he was awarded a five year contract and he left supporters with some memorable moments without being able to win promotion from the lower divisions.

However, it must be said, it was extremely difficult to win promotion from the regional Third Divisions when only one club went up. However, City became founder members of the new national Third Division when the regional Third Divisions were scrapped in 1958 – the top 12 clubs formed the Third Division, the bottom 12 the Division Four. However, City were facing relegation from the Third Division when they sacked him in March 1961. Jackson will be remembered for two outstanding FA Cup runs – reaching the fifth round before being knocked out by Burnley after a replay at Turf Moor in 1959-60 and reaching the fourth round before being beaten by Preston the season before. City's best league placing under Jackson was in the last season of Third Division North in 1957-8. He will be remembered for some bargain signings, among them Bobby Webb, Les Samuels, Johnny Simm, David Boyle, Jim Lawlor, Tom Flockett, David Layne and, from Scotland, John McCole, Malcolm Currie, Willie Marshall, Billy Barnes and John Reid as well as developing young players like Derek Stokes, Trevor Hockey and Bruce Stowell.

BOB'S TWO NEAR MISSES

Bob Brocklebank could be known as the 'nearly man.' In his three seasons at Valley Parade, the club twice narrowly missed promotion from the Fourth Division, finishing fifth in 1961-2 and 1963-4 with a re-election application in between. The former Aston Villa and Burnley player, arrived at Valley Parade in 1961 with a wealth of managerial experience at Chesterfield, Birmingham City and Hull City, but, like so many of his post war counterparts could not find success at Valley Parade. After a poor first half of season in 1961-2, City embarked on a remarkable run of success in the last three months of the campaign, winning 15 of their last 19 matches and losing only two. A winning run began with a 2-0 win at Accrington Stanley, but that's where City were out of luck because, three weeks later, Stanley went out of business and all points gained against were deducted. City's bad start to the season left them no margin for error and they suffered what proved to be a crucial 5-3 defeat at Workington in the next to the last match of the season and, although they recovered to beat Wrexham 5-3 in the last match, they missed out on promotion.

The season will be remembered for the goal scoring exploits of David 'Bronco' Layne, who scored a club record 34 League goals, but Brocklebank was forced to sell him in the close season to Sheffield Wednesday, did not adequately replace him and the new look side flopped so badly that they finished next to the bottom of the table and had to apply for re-election. Brocklebank found another goal scoring centre forward midway through that season, Halifax born Rodney Green from Bradford Park Avenue and he scored 29 League goals as City once more finished in fifth place. Hopes rose as they won five matches in a row with a 2-1 victory at Lincoln City on Easter Monday and a 17,974 crowd gathered at Valley Parade to see them play Workington, knowing that a win would see them promoted. Unfortunately, City flopped on the big occasion, losing 2-0 to their rivals and the chance was gone. Brocklebank was forced to sell Green during the summer to Gillingham and, although the directors extended his contract for another two years, he resigned after a poor start to the 1964-5 season.

DOUBLE INTERNATIONAL IN CHARGE

A lower division club in Yorkshire looking for a so-called big name manager need look no further than double international Willie Watson, who joined them in April 1966. A wing half or inside forward, Watson, who played wartime football for his father's old club Huddersfield Town, joined Sunderland after the war and played eight seasons with them in the old First Division. He was capped by England in a Victory international against Wales and gained four full England caps as well as playing in B internationals. He was chosen in the 1950 World cup party, but never played. In October 1954 he was made player manager of Halifax Town, but left to concentrate on cricket. He re-joined them ten years later as manager, but they had to apply for re-election to the Fourth Division and it was a surprise when Stafford Heginbotham's board invited him to become City's manager in succession to Bill Harris. He stabilised the club after their third re-election application in 1966 and laid the foundations for their promotion in 1969.

In fact, City were on course for a strong promotion bid – they missed out by one place – when he surprised supporters by resigning in January 1968 to take over as sports administrator of the Wanderers Club in Johannesburg. Watson spent six years with the Wanderers before over a poultry farm and he died in South Africa in 2004 aged 84. Watson made 211 League appearances at football, but was better known to many people as a successful cricketer. A left handed batsman, he scored more than 14,000 runs for Yorkshire before joining Leicestershire for whom he scored 7,000 runs and became captain and assistant secretary as well as an England selector. He played in 23 Test matches and hit two centuries, including 109 when he saved a Test match against Australia in 1953 in a long partnership with Trevor Bailey. Heginbotham always introduced him as 'the man who saved England.'

TRAGEDY STRIKES AS MANAGER DIES

Tragedy struck Valley Parade on Thursday, March 7, 1968 when recently appointed manager Grenville Hair collapsed after taking a training session at the ground and was dead on arrival at hospital. Hair was only 36 and it was great shock that someone so and apparently fit should die so young. Hair, who joined City in February 1967 after spending three years as player manager of Wellington Town later Telford United. Well respected by the players, he was a natural choice to succeed Willie Watson when the manager resigned in January 1968, but he had no time to prove himself and had been in the job for only six weeks when he died. Less than 24 hours earlier, Hair had negotiated a controversial double exchange transfer deal with neighbours Huddersfield Town. The deal brought Town's right back Denis Atkins and centre forward Tony Leighton plus £15,000 to Valley Parade while City right back Alex Smith and centre forward Paul Aimson joined Huddersfield. Hair, who was born at Burton-on-Trent, signed for Leeds United in May 1948, one of manager Major Buckley's young players. A left back, he played in United's Second Division promotion team in 1955-6 in a successful partnership with Scottish right back Jimmy Dunn.

Hair, whose wife Jill worked in the City pools office, made 474 League and cup appearances for Leeds before joining Wellington. Tributes came from many quarters among them former Leeds United manager Don

ROBBIE BLAKE - GOAL SCORING HERO OF CITY'S PROMOTION TO THE PREMIER LEAGUE

Revie and team mate John Charles. Revie said: "I will never forget how Grenville fought to keep Leeds United out of the Third Division when I started out as a manager. Everybody was hoping he would achieve big things as a manager. We were all deeply shocked at this tragic news from Valley Parade. Charles said: "Grenville and I joined Leeds United in the same week and went into the army together on the same day. He was a wonderful soccer companion, dedicated to the game and always loyal and sincere."

FATHER OWEN ARRIVES

After Grenville Hair's tragic death coach Jimmy McAnearney assisted by skipper Tom Hallett took charge of the side until the end of the 1967-8, which ended in disappointment as City finished fifth, one place outside the top four Fourth Division promotion places for the third time in seven years. The directors decided to make a fresh start and appointed long serving Reading assistant Jimmy Wheeler as manager. Reading, who was born at Reading, made 406 League appearances for his home-town club, scoring 147 goals. A broken leg at Barnsley in September 1964, effectively ended his first team career, but he captained and coached the reserve side with success, leading them to the Football Combination Second Division title in 1966-7 when he was elected Reading's player of the year. He enjoyed immediate success at City, leading the club to promotion from the Fourth Division in his first season – 1968-9 – and City were well placed for another promotion midway through the following season after an 8-1 thrashing of Bournemouth on the fourth Saturday of January 1970, but City won only three of their last 20 matches to finish a disappointing tenth. Clearly, the team needed strengthening and Stafford Heginbotham's board of directors decided on a bold move to sell Valley Parade to Bradford Council for £35,000 and lease it back at £3,500 a year. The cash raised was to be used for team strengthening and Wheeler used it to buy strikers Colin Hall from Nottingham Forest and Terry Own, father of England striker Michael Owen, from Everton where he had been a reserve player.

Unfortunately, neither was a success, Hall scoring a mere seven goals in 72 League and cup appearances over two years before being transferred to Bristol City and Owen also scoring only seven goals 57 League and cup appearances also over two years before he left to enjoy a long and successful career with Chester. City struggled in Wheeler's third season, finishing a disappointing 19th and, when they made a bad start to the following campaign, he left following 7-1 thrashing at Bristol Rovers in only the fifth match of the season despite being only 18 months into a five year contract.

WORLD CUP HERO AT HELM

He was manager for only two months, but England World Cup hero Ray Wilson made a big impression and there was disappointment among City supporters when he decided to walk away from football and join the family undertakers' business in Huddersfield. Wilson joined City from Oldham Athletic as player coach in July 1970 and made two League appearances the following season, but injury forced him to call time on his playing career and he concentrated on coaching. He was placed in charge of the team as caretaker manager when Jimmy Wheeler and had a good response from the players as City embarked on a mini-revival with five wins during his two months in charge, but, despite pleas from directors, players and supporters for him to stay on Valley Parade as manager, Wilson was adamant he wanted to leave and pursue another career. A left back, Wilson made 266 League appearances for Huddersfield Town, where his full back partner for part of the time was future City player Denis Atkins before moving to Everton. It was while he played at Everton that he won a World Cup winner's medal with England, playing in the 4-2 win over West Germany at Wembley in 1966. He made 116 League appearances before winding down his career at Oldham and then with City.

When Ray Wilson left City, the club turned to the former Bolton Wanderers player, Bryan Edwards, who was then assistant manager at Plymouth Argyle. Unfortunately, he could not save City from relegation and they finished bottom of Division Three after a dreadful run of results in the second half of the season, in which they won only three of their last 24 matches and scored a mere 11 goals in final 20 games. Relegation after only three seasons back in the Third Division was a blow to the club, but, with funds in short supply, it was clear there would be quick return to Division Three as City finished 16th and eighth in the following two seasons and Edward sacked in January 1975 after three and a half seasons in charge with the club in a promising sixth place. However, that wasn't the end of Edwards' association with City for, after training as a physiotherapist, he worked as a coach and physiotherapist at Huddersfield Town and youth team coach at Leeds United before returning to Valley Parade as part of their backroom staff. He was appointed general manager in May 1978, working with one of his signings, former Northern Ireland international defender John Napier and assistant manager and physiotherapist when George Mulhall became manager. He continued as physiotherapist under succeeding managers and following his retirement in recent years he has worked at Valley Parade as match day host. As a player, Leeds born Edwards was a one club man, playing 18 years with Bolton Wanderers mainly as a wing half and later as a centre half, making 483 League appearances, most of them in the top division. The highlight was winning an FA Cup winner's medal against Manchester United in

1958. He left in 1965, aged 35, and became assistant trainer coach at Blackpool. He became coach at Preston in 1969 and later first team trainer before moving to Plymouth as chief coach. A noted cricketer, Edwards was invited for trial with Yorkshire before deciding to concentrate on professional football. After joining City, he played in the Bradford League with Bradford CC at Park Avenue.

PROMOTION FOR KENNEDY

When City sacked Bryan Edward, they turned to youth team manager Bobby Kennedy to take charge and the enjoyed two successful seasons under the former Scotland under-23 international before he too was sacked in January 1978.

In his first full season, City reached the quarter final of the FA Cup for the first time for 56 years, but were beaten 1-0 by the eventual winners Southampton in a tense match at Valley Parade. Unfortunately, City flopped in the league after their cup exit and finished a disappointing 17th. However, the following season, with additions to the squad, City managed to win promotion back to Division Three, finishing in the fourth promotion place, building on a good start to the season and surviving a dip in the middle of the campaign before finishing strongly with only two defeats in the last 12 matches as promotion was achieved in the next to the last match of the campaign. Unfortunately, City were not able to recruit sufficiently well to meet the demands of the new division and, after winning only six of their first 26 matches, Kennedy was sacked two days after a 4-1 defeat at Cambridge United – their fifth defeat in a row – in what was also Ron Atkinson's last match in charge before he moved to West Bromwich Albion. Kennedy's dismissal split the board as two directors, Jack Tordoff and Trevor Davidson resigned in protest. A wing half, Kennedy made his name in Scotland with Kilmarnock, playing in their Scottish Cup and First Division runners-up team in 1959-60 and the following season he collected runners-up medals in both the League and Scottish League Cup. His form attracted the attention of English scouts and in July 1961 he moved to Manchester City for £42,500 – then a record fee between Scottish and English clubs. He experienced promotion and relegation during eight years at Manchester City although he did not play enough games to qualify for a League Championship medal when City won the title in 1967-8. After making 254 League and cup games at home and in European competitions, Kennedy joined Grimsby Town as player manager in March 1969 for £9,000. He could not prevent Grimsby from having to apply for re-election and after making 88 first appearances for the Mariners. He resigned in May 1971. After leaving City he spent four months as coach with Blackburn Rovers he left football for good, but continued to live in the Bradford area while he and his wife Barbara were involved in a clothing business in Manchester. Their daughter Lorraine was played football for many years and represented Scotland's in women's soccer internationals. Their son Graham is a member of City's youth coaching team. John Napier, one of Bryan Edwards' key signings, when he joined City from Bolton in October 1972, the Northern Ireland international central defender brought a touch of class to the defence in 118 League and cup appearances, but he was less successful when the club appointed him as manager to succeed Bobby Kennedy in February 1978. He had been a coach under Kennedy, but even though he had the help of Edwards, who had returned to work in the Valley Parade backroom staff, he struggled to cope with his new role and parted company in October 1978 after only eight months at the helm. Napier went to America to play in NASL with Philadelphia Furies as well as working as a coach at soccer camps in the United States.

MULHALL TAKES OVER

Having appointed a novice manager in John Napier, City turned to an experienced campaigner when chairman Bob Martin persuaded his friend, George Mulhall to become Napier's successor in November 1978. The club had tried to persuade Mulhall to join them ten months earlier when Bobby Kennedy was sacked, but he decided to stay with Bolton where he was assistant to former Huddersfield Town boss Ian Greaves and he helped Greaves to guide the club to the Second Division championship that 1977-8 season. He stabilised the club in his first season before making developing what looked like a promotion side in 1979-80. Two important close season signings, centre forward David Staniforth from Bristol Rovers and defender Terry Cooper from Lincoln teamed up with key players like defender Steve Baines, two former Leeds United players, striker David McNiven and midfield player Mick Bates, new goalkeeper Steve Smith, Mick Wood, Ces Podd, Garry Watson, Terry Dolan, Don Hutchins and Lammie Robertson and then, midway through the campaign came start signing Bobby Campbell. City made a great start with seven wins in their first eight matches and were in a promotion position for most of the season, but they failed at the final hurdle. The Bantams went into their last match at Peterborough needing only to draw to be sure of finishing fourth, but they lost 1-0 in flat performance and four other results went against them as finished fifth. The following season was an anti-climax and it was no surprise when Mulhall left the following March to go back to Bolton as assistant manager.

He later became manager and was also assistant to former Bolton favourite Frank Worthington at Tranmere Rovers. A Scotland international winger, Mulhall began his career with Aberdeen before joining Sunderland in 1962 in a £25,000 deal. He scored 66 goals in 284 League and cup games for Sunderland, helping them to promotion to the First Division before winding down his playing career in South Africa in a two-year spell with Cape Town City. He then became trainer coach of Halifax Town and then manager at the Shay before beginning his association with Bolton. He has also enjoyed managerial roles at Halifax in more recent years.

DOC'S REMEDY FAILS TO CURE

After calling time on Terry Yorath's 13 month management spell in March 1989, the City directors turned to a manager with a different style of play to try to stave off the threat of relegation back to the Third Division. City were in grave danger of relegation when former Millwall manager John Docherty arrived at Valley Parade and, although he enjoyed a morale boosting 3-2 home win over Newcastle United in his first match in charge, he couldn't prevent City from sliding back to Division Three at the end of a miserable campaign. The fans enjoyed Yorath's passing style of play, but City lacked a cutting edge, which meant that wins were few and far between. A winger, Docherty, who had three spells with Brentford besides playing for Sheffield United and Reading in a 14-year career as a player, had led Millwall to the Second Division championship two years earlier. He was an unashamed apostle of a more direct approach, which the City fans hated and, as this style didn't achieve results either, the club were left with the worst of both worlds. Docherty's immediate task once relegation had been confirmed was the cut the wage bill and recoup some money in the transfer market under instructions from chairman David Simpson and his board. So, out went many of Yorath's signings, often at less than City paid for them, including Ian McCall to Dunfermline, Neil Woods to Grimsby, Dave Evans to Halifax, Alan Davies back to Swansea, Peter Jackson to Huddersfield and eventually Tony Adcock, who returned to Northampton.

In that respect he did a good job for the club and he also made a shrewd signing when he brought in striker Sean McCarthy from Plymouth in a £250,000 deal and former Welsh international Robbie James in part exchange for Davies. His other signings were mainly from his old club Millwall with only Phil Babb and Stephen Torpey making much impact. The only way Docherty, assisted by former Welsh international Leighton James, could win over the fans was by success on the field, but they finished eighth in his only full season and when they made a bad start to the following campaign, the unpopular manager paid the price.

THE LAWRENCE ERA

The experienced Lennie Lawrence was new chairman Geoffrey Richmond's first managerial appointment in May 1994. He wasn't first choice. Richmond had tried and failed to tempt Port Vale manager John

Rudge, but he decided to stay at Vale Park, but Lawrence came a fine pedigree, having made his name during a long spell at Charlton Athletic before moving north to Middlesbrough. He had won promotion to the Premier League with Boro, but they had been relegated after just one season in the top flight and the club decided not to renew his contract at the end of his three year deal. Lawrence was given money to spend, breaking the club's transfer record by signing striker John Taylor from Bristol Rovers for £300,000 defender Jon Ford from Swansea for £210,000 in his first season and, in his second season he bought three players from Leicester City, Gavin Ward, Nicky Mohan and Ian Ormondroyd in a deal valued at £475,000 on the same day. He also sold defender Dean Richards to Wolves and Taylor to Luton after less than a season at Valley Parade. However, despite some success in the League Cup there was nothing in City's league form to suggest that City were going to gain the promotion that Richmond craved. So, Lawrence was sacked in November 1995 after 18 months in charge, but, as he pointed out later, his sacking by City had no effect on his managerial career. He was appointed manager of Luton three weeks later and has since managed at Grimsby, Cardiff and Bristol Rovers and is one of select few managers to have managed in more than 1,000 games.

KAMARA TAKES CHARGE

Lawrence's successor at Valley Parade was his No 2 Chris Kamara. The much travelled midfield player was one of Lawrence's first signings – from Sheffield United – but his long playing career tailed off after one season when he was promoted to assistant manager. He was manager at Valley Parade for a little over two years, but what an eventful period that was as he guided City to the play-offs after a good late run enabled them to snatch sixth place in the table and then an unforgettable day in the play-off final at the old Wembley stadium where they beat Notts County 2-0 to win promotion with his key signing Matt Stallard scoring the second goal. In his second season, he brought in a string of foreign along with former England, Newcastle, Tottenham, Sheffield Wednesday and Marseilles winger Chris Waddle as City managed to hang on to their First Division status by winning their last two matches against Charlton and Queens Park Rangers in a dramatic end of season. However, he was sacked midway through the following season when results were not to chairman Geoffrey Richmond's liking. He joined his old club Stoke City as manager soon after leaving Valley Parade, but that appointment lasted a matter of weeks and since then he has forged a successful career as a Sky TV football commentator and presenter. In a 20-year career, Kamara played for Portsmouth, Sheffield Untied and Swindon twice, Brentford, Stoke, Leeds United, Luton and Middlesbrough with 641 League appearances and 71 goals.

Chris Hutchings was appointed City manager in June 2000 after Paul Jewell after surprise resignation of Paul Jewell after one season in the Premier League and presided over the spending spree, dubbed the summer of madness. Hutchings, who played first arrived at City as reserve team coach, but succeeded Gary Megson as first team coach in December 1995 when Megson left to become manager at Norwich. However, after City gained promotion through the play-offs in 1996, manager Chris Kamara brought in Martin Hunter to become first team coach and Hutchings was asked to work with the youth teams. Hutchings was disappointed at this apparent demotion, but took pride in bringing young players through and when Paul Jewell succeeded Karma in 1998, he asked Hutchings to become his assistant.

The two of them led City to promotion the following year and then masterminded Premier League survival in 2000. Then, when Jewell resigned in June 2000, chairman Geoffrey Richmond turned to Hutchings. He was manager at Valley Parade for less than five months, but an eventful spell it was in the club's history. First, he led them in the Inter-Toto Cup campaign, and then he presided over the spending spree that led to the recruitment of Benito Carbone, Dan Petrescu, David Hopkin, Peter Atherton, Ian Nolan, Ashley Ward and finally Stan Collymore. As Hutchings pointed out later, it was not so much the fees that City paid in respect of Hopkin £2.5 million, Petrescu £1 million and Ward £1.5 million, but the wages for such as Carbone – reported to be on £40,000 a week – and Petrescu which led to City paying some £13 million in wages in their second Premier League season. Unfortunately for Hutchings, results on the field went against him despite this unprecedented investment in the team and he was sacked in the first week of November with City next to the bottom of the table having gone ten matches without a win. Despite this setback, Hutchings stayed in management, teaming up again with Paul Jewell as his No 2 in a successful spell at Wigan Athletic and is now manage of League One club Walsall. During his playing career, Winchester born Hutchings made 468 League appearances with Chelsea, Brighton, Huddersfield Town, Walsall and Rotherham in a 13-year career.

JEFFERIES MOVES SOUTH

Chairman Geoffrey Richmond sprang a surprise when he turned to Jim Jefferies as Chris Hutchings' successor in November 2000. Jefferies was a well known name in Scotland having managed Berwick, Falkirk and Hearts over a 12-year period, but had never managed south of the border. His task was to keep City in the Premier League, but the team had gained only seven points from their first 14 matches and the task proved beyond him. And, so the Bantams were relegated with 26 points, ten points less than the previous season when they stayed up by beating Liverpool on the final day of the campaign. Statistics tell the story of a miserable campaign – just five wins from 38 matches with the £40,000 a week Italian Benito Carbone the top scorer with a paltry five goals.

City began the new season in the First Division with a 4-0 home win over Barnsley – two penalties from Ashley Ward and other goals from Eoin Jess and Carbone – but overall results were poor in the first half of the new campaign and, with only nine wins from their first 27 matches to start of the New Year, it was no surprise that Jefferies handed in his resignation on Christmas Eve three days after his trusted No 2 Billy Brown had also resigned. Jefferies return to Scotland and within weeks he and Brown were installed as the managerial team at Kilmarnock. They stayed there until midway through the 2009-10 season when they left and soon after that were back in management at Hearts. In fact, Jefferies had resigned as manager Hearts only a fortnight before taking the City job.

THE LAWMAN COMETH

Chesterfield manager Nicky Law was City's choice as manager to succeed Jim Jefferies and he took over on 31st December 2001. Chairman Geoffrey Richmond had been impressed by Law's achievement in guiding Chesterfield to promotion, but his first task at Valley Parade was to ensure that City survived in the First Division following their relegation from the Premier League the previous season. He managed to do that, but no sooner had the season ended that he and everyone else connected with the club were hit by the new that City were going into administration. The club's future hung in the balance during a tense summer at the end of which Richmond left the club to be succeeded by theme park boss Gordon Gibb, whose family owned Flamingo Land in North Yorkshire with Julian Rhodes as chief executive. Law also had to cope with the aftermath of Benito Carbone returning to Italy with a £1 million pay-out instead of his full entitlement. There followed a difficult season for Law as City used 35 players, including four goalkeepers and was also handicapped by injuries to experienced players like David Wetherall, Ashley Ward and Peter Atherton. They had a dreadful first half of season, which featured seven successive defeats, including home defeats, against Wimbledon 5-3 and Stuart McCall's Sheffield United 5-0.

The season was rescued by some fine away wins, including one at Wolves just after Christmas, Ipswich, Coventry and Burnley, but once survival had been achieved, the season ended on a flat note with four successive defeats with no goals concluding with a 5-0 thrashing at home to Portsmouth on the last day of the season. Law gave first team chances to 18-year-olds Lewis Emanuel and Danny Forrest and discovered Simon Francis, who was released by Nottingham Forest. Andy Gray, who joined City from Nottingham Forest, was top scorer with 15 goals while Danish midfield player Claus Jorgensen scored 11. City made a bad start to the following season, losing ten of their first 18 matches and after they were held to a 1-1 home draw against fellow strugglers Walsall in November Law was sacked. Law, who began his career at Arsenal, played with Barnsley, Plymouth, Notts County, Scarborough, Rotherham and Chesterfield where he became manager and Hereford. After leaving City he became manager of Grimsby, but when they were relegated he suffered the indignity of being sacked for the second time in a season. He returned to management in Northern Counties East League with Alfreton, but his connection with City continued when his son Nicky spent time on loan spells with the club in 2007-08 and 2008-09 while he was a Sheffield United player, but he turned down their offer of a contract in the summer of 2009 and joined Rotherham.

NO SUCCESS FOR CAPTAIN MARVEL

Former England international captain Bryan Robson was City's big name successor to Nicky Law, but the appointment was not a success. The former Manchester United and West Brom midfield lasted only six months after arriving at Valley Parade in November 2003, resigning at the end of the 2003-04 season during the administration crisis as City were relegated. Robson, dubbed Captain Marvel after years as captain of England and Manchester United – 90 caps, 65 of them as captain and three World Cup campaigns with his country, FA Cup and top flight Championship glory and a European Cup Winners' medal with United. After more than 450 appearances and 97 goals with United, Robson left to become player manager of Middlesbrough and had a roller coaster experience during his five years at the Riverside. He guided Boro into the Premier League as First Division champions in his first season.

During the following year Boro lost in the League Cup final after a replay. The team were relegated from the Premier League, but reached the FA Cup final only to lose to Chelsea. The following season they were promoted straight back to the Premier League and reached the League Cup final again only to lose one again – to Chelsea. Robson was rewarded with a five years contract, but it started going wrong after that even though Robson continued to keep Boro in the Premier League, finishing ninth and 12th in successive seasons. The board brought in former England manager Terry Venables as head coach for six months and, even though Boro finished eight points clear of the relegation zone in 2001, Robson left the club. City's decision to make him manager was a surprise. Another candidate, Colin Todd, who spent a successful six months as coach at Valley Parade when Frank Stapleton was player manager, was named as his No 2 and he suggested the two men would complement each other. City won their first match 3-2 against Millwall in front of the Sky TV cameras at Valley Parade after a dramatic fightback, the winning goal coming in stoppage time through substitute Michael Branch after goals from Danny Cadamarteri and Andy Gray had put them back in the game. But that's as good as it got for Robson as City lost their next five matches. Defeat in the FA Cup at Second Division Luton followed and, although there were bright spots like a 1-0 home win over Coventry at Christmas and a 1-0 win at eventual champions Norwich, City won only one of their last nine matches and ended their miserable season with five successive defeats. Robson, who brought in several loan players, was handicapped when City went into administration in February 2004 and lost three key players as the administrators sold Gray and Simon Francis to Sheffield United, Gray for £60,000 and Francis for £200,000 while Welsh international Paul Evans went to Nottingham Forest for £35,000. Robson made it clear that would not continue as manager if City were still in financial trouble and resigned during the summer.

No manager could have had a tougher start to a season than Colin Todd when he took over from Bryan Robson at the end of June 2004. For, he had only eight senior players, up to 14 players having taken up the advice of the administrators to get fixed up with other clubs. Originally, Todd had been appointed as assistant to Bryan Robson, but Robson made it clear he did not want to be manager in the new season if City were still in administration so in stepped Todd. The former England and Derby County defender turned to be just the man to guide City through this traumatic period in the club's when their future was in considerable doubt. City lost several key players during that anxious summer, but striker Dean Windass remained after seriously thinking about Darlington's offer of a player coach role and he made a huge contribution with 28 goals while other experienced players – David Wetherall, Wayne Jacobs, Peter Atherton and Mike Summerbee stayed and he signed Darren Holloway from MK Dons, Lee Crooks from Barnsley, Everton youngsters Michael Symes and Steve Schumacher and goalkeepers Paul Henderson and Donovan Ricketts, Todd not only steadied the ship as City came out of administration for the second time, but was left feeling disappointed that the Bantams had not made the play-offs.

He continued as manager during the following season before being sacked by chairman Julian Rhodes in February 2007 when poor results suggested that City would not make the play-offs again. David Wetherall succeeded him as caretaker manager, but results got worse as City suffered their third relegation in six years as they slid to the fourth tier of English football for the first time for 25 years, paving the way for the return of Stuart McCall. Born at Chester le Street in County Durham, Todd enjoyed an illustrious playing career spanning 18 years that began in 10966 with Sunderland before he won League championship honours at in an eight year spell at Derby County under Brian Clough as central defensive partner to Roy McFarland. He gained 27 England caps and made 641 League appearances, 173 with Sunderland and 293 with Derby before he moved to Everton, Birmingham City, Nottingham Forest, Oxford and Luton. He also played in Canada for Vancouver. His managerial and coaching career included spells at Middlesbrough, Bolton and Derby. After leaving City, Todd had a spell as manager in Denmark and he was manager of Darlington in the first few weeks of the 2009-10 season before he and assistant, former City striker Dean Windass were sacked because of poor results.

After Stuart McCall's departure in February 2010, City turned to one of the most experienced managers in business as his successor. The sheer breadth of Peter Taylor's CV makes impressive reading. From managing England under-21s down the divisions to the non-League, the 57-year-old Taylor has experienced most things in football. A winger, he made 388 appearances, scoring 87 goals in a playing career that began with his town club Southend United and continued at Crystal Palace, Sours, Leyton Orient, Exeter City and on loan with Oldham Athletic. He also won four England caps in 1976. In management, he has enjoyed two spells in charge of England under-21s and also managed the full national for one match – in Italy – as caretaker following the sudden resignation of Kevin Keegan in 2000 when he handed David Beckham the captain's armband. His club career has taken in spells at Dartford, Southend, Dover Athletic, Gillingham, Leicester City, Brighton, Hull City, Crystal Palace, Stevenage, Wycombe and now Bradford City.

Most City supporters have focussed on his four year spell at Hull between 2002 and 2006 when he won two promotions, leading them out of the bottom division in his full season, 2002-03 and then to the Championship – the second tier of English football – the following season. They were also impressed with his achievement of leading Wycombe out of the bottom division in 2008-09. After a promising start to his Valley Parade career, Taylor signed a one-year contract and, after extensive close-season recruiting, hopes were high that he could win promotion with City in 2010-11. Sadly, that was not the case. Taylor resigned at the end of February 2011 with the team stuck in the bottom half of the table and it was left to former City defender Peter Jackson to guide the club to League Two safety with four wins in the last two months of the season, one of them a dramatic 2-1 success against Rotherham United on a tense night at Valley Parade. The match had moved into stoppage time when Tom Adeyemi, a teenage midfield player on loan from Norwich City, tried his luck with a 30-yard shot, which struck the underside of the crossbar. Many in the crowd did not think the ball had crossed the line, but the referee ruled that it had and City gained a priceless three points towards survival. However, safety from relegation was not achieved until three matches from the end with a 2-1 home win over Aldershot – and the unhappy season ended with a humiliating 5-1 home defeat at the hands of Crewe.

JACKSON'S DEPARTURE

The big question when the season was over was would Peter Jackson continue as manager? Initially, Jackson, who had enjoyed experience as manager of Huddersfield Town with whom he gained promotion and also at Lincoln City, offered to step in as interim manager and try to guide the club to League Two safety. Was he the longer-term answer as manager? What did the directors think? Well it took them three weeks before confirming him as manager and City embarked on a close-season drive aided by Archie Christie, appointed chief scout and head of development – a new post for Bradford City. It was all to end in tears. Despite extensive close-season recruiting, much of it instigated by Christie, City took only one point from their first four matches. The directors were not impressed and when he attended a weekly board meeting Jackson was challenged on the start to the season. Upset by the criticism from some of the directors, the manager said words to the effect that if that was what they thought, he would offer to resign. He was asked to leave the room and when he was recalled to the meeting some 20 minutes later, he was told the directors accepted his resignation.

PARKINSON STEPS INTO BREACH

Some supporters expected City to appoint Jackson's impressive No 2, the former Middlesbrough player and coach, Colin Cooper, but although he won his only match in charge, the directors decided to go for the experienced Phil Parkinson and what an inspired appointment they made. Parkinson, who arrived at Valley Parade with eight years' managerial experience with Colchester United, Hull City and Charlton Athletic behind him, had been linked with the Valley Parade job before. Now he faced the task of lifting the so-called sleeping giant from the depths of League Two without the opportunity of working with the players in pre-season while inheriting another manager's close-season signings. Parkinson began to bring in his own players, including winger Kyel Reid and loan signings, among them defender Andrew Davies, but, not surprisingly, the team struggled for consistency. They didn't secure their place in the League until three matches from the end with a 1-0 home win over Macclesfield and finished in the same position as the season before – a disappointing 18th, seventh from the bottom.

One of the few highlights was reaching the northern semi-final of the Johnstone's Paint Trophy following impressive victories over local rivals Huddersfield Town and the two Sheffield clubs, Wednesday and United, only to lose at Oldham in the semi-final. In truth, no one expected too much from Parkinson's first season, but most people had confidence in an experienced manager, who had enjoyed an impressive playing career, making more than 500 appearances with two clubs Bury and Reading. He was particularly popular during his 11 seasons at Reading, being voted player of the season two seasons in a row, 1997-98 and 1998-99, a member of the 1993-94 Second Division championship side, captaining the team to promotion from the Second Division in 2001-02 and being awarded a testimonial before retiring in 2002-03. Parkinson went straight into management after leaving Reading, joining Colchester in February 2003 and leading them to promotion in 2005-06 when they finished in second place in League One despite having the lowest attendances in the division. He resigned in June 2006 with a year of his contract left to join Hull City as manager following the departure of future City manager Peter Taylor. However, his brief spell at Hull was not successful and he left after only five months in charge with Hull in the relegation zone having won only five of his 24 matches in charge. Parkinson joined Charlton Athletic in January 2007 as assistant manager to Alan Pardew, later Newcastle United manager, the pair having previously worked together at Reading. He was close to a return to management with Huddersfield Town in April 2007, but made a last-minute decision to remain at Charlton. He later extended his contract with Charlton until 2010 following Pardew's departure in November 2008. He was first appointed caretaker manager and was given the job permanently on New Year's Eve. Under his management Charlton were relegated to the third tier of English football, but the following season Parkinson led Charlton to the play-offs only to lose 5-4 on penalties to Swindon after the two-legged semi-final had finished 3-3 on aggregate. He was sacked midway through the following season – January 2011 – after a bad run of results. He returned to management with Bradford City in August of that year.

A SEASON OF SUPERLATIVES

What words can describe the 2012-13 season – all superlatives surely – momentous, unprecedented, historic, outstanding – add your own, I'm sure they will fit the bill. For Bradford City followers, whose team had spent six seasons in League Two – the old Fourth Division – and for the previous two seasons had only narrowly escaped being relegated to non-league, to play at Wembley twice in the space of three months was like living in dreamland. Above all, after tumbling down from the Premier League to League Two between 2001 and 2007, this was the season when the club's fightback began. City gained worldwide publicity for their

achievement in reaching the Capital One League Cup Final after beating three Premier League teams – Wigan Athletic, Arsenal and Aston Villa – along the way before crashing 5-0 against Swansea at Wembley. However, it was their second Wembley appearance – and their 3-0 win against Northampton in the League Two final – that will hopefully have more long-term implications.

The story of this extraordinary season began a week before the start of the regular campaign. City and Notts County agreed to play their Capital One first round cup tie at Meadow Lane on Saturday 11 August and City, fielding six summer signings, gained a somewhat surprising 1-0 win thanks to a goal in extra time by James Hanson. It was a notable victory against a team one division higher than them, but no one could possibly have forecast that seven months later they would be playing in the final at Wembley in front of 82,000 spectators. Their next League Cup test was another away trip, this time to Championship team Watford, managed by former Chelsea favourite Gianfranco Zola – potentially an even more difficult challenge than the first round tie at Meadow Lane. City went into the match with confidence after two consecutive home wins, including a 5-1 triumph over AFC Wimbledon. Parkinson made changes, leaving key players like Kyel Reid, James Hanson and Nathan Doyle on the bench, but all three were introduced in the second half. The odds were against City when Watford went in front after 71 minutes, but Reid equalised after 84 minutes and Garry Thompson scored a dramatic last-minute winner to send the Bantams through to the third round. On the face of it, a home tie against Burton Albion from City's own division presented an easier task than Notts County and Watford away, but it didn't turn out like that when the Brewers came to Valley Parade in the last week in September.

In fact, Burton were leading 2-0 until seven minutes from the end when Wells, who came on as a double substitute with Hanson after 61 minutes, pulled a goal back after 83 minutes before sending the tie into extra time with a last-minute equaliser. Then right-back Stephen Darby – not normally known as a goalscorer – scored the winner with a 30-yard shot just inside the near post with five minutes of extra time left. Having reached the fourth round of the League Cup, City had high hopes of a lucrative home draw against a leading Premier League club. That would come later in the competition. In the meantime, they were drawn away to Wigan Athletic – a Premier League club, but not the glamorous tie the club had in mind. As it happened, the match at the DW Stadium turned out to be a memorable occasion for the magnificent turnout of 5,000 visiting fans, making up almost half of the disappointing 11,777 crowd as the Bantams reached the last eight of the League Cup for the first time in 24 years. Manager Phil Parkinson recalled keeper Matt Duke, who had not played in the previous eight games and made changes to cover the absence through injury and suspension of Andrew Davies, Luke Oliver and Ricky Ravenhill. The loss of key defenders Davies and Oliver was a particular blow. So, Rory McArdle switched to the centre of defence with Irish teenager Carl McHugh, starting only his third game, lining up alongside him.

After some early scares, wingers Zavon Hines and Garry Thompson dropped back effectively to make a back six to frustrate City's Premier League opponents. The Bantams created few chances, but equally they restricted Wigan to only a handful of opportunities and the result was deadlock, a goalless draw after extra time and so to penalties. Nathan Doyle, substitute Gary Jones and Stephen Darby converted their spot kicks while David Jones and Ben Watson were also successful for Wigan, but, when substitute Alan Connell put City 4-2 in front, the pressure was on Jordi Gomez. Fortunately for City, Duke was equal to the task and saved the Spanish player's spot kick to spark wild scenes of celebration among players and fans. "I am ecstatic," said Phil Parkinson, speaking for everyone connected with the club. "I thought the discipline of the team was top-drawer. It shows what can be done with big hearts and discipline and if everyone sticks to their jobs." The quarter-final draw gave just the plum tie that City wanted – Arsenal at home on Tuesday 11 December in front of the Sky TV cameras and a near-capacity crowd of 23,971, including 4,500 Arsenal fans. And what a night it was for the home supporters as the Bantams won 3-2 on penalties after extra time to go through to the semi-final.

Manager Arsene Wenger, who so often has played understrength sides in the League Cup to give opportunities to his talented young players, fielded a strong side for Arsenal's first visit to Valley Parade since City's two Premier League seasons. One sensed that to have any chance of beating Arsenal's star-studded team City would have to score first and give themselves something to defend and so it happened in the 16th minute. Nahki Wells was brought down, and Gary Jones's free kick was flicked on by Will Atkinson for Garry Thompson to score. Remarkably, City frustrated Arsenal to such an extent that they were only three minutes away from a famous victory when Arsenal equalised with a header from captain Vermaelen to send the tie into extra time. The Gunners hit the crossbar in extra time, but somehow City survived to take part in another penalty shoot-out and more drama.

Scores by Nathan Doyle and Gary Jones and two misses by Arsenal gave City a 2-0 lead in the penalty shoot-out, but then Stephen Darby missed and Jack Wilshere scored to give Arsenal some hope at 2-1. Alan Connell made it 3-1 before Alex Oxlade-Chamberlain kept Arsenal in the tie at 3-2. Unfortunately, substitute Ritchie Jones stretched supporters' nerves to breaking point when he missed the chance to win the tie for City before Vermaelen became the second visiting penalty taker to hit the post amid scenes of wild celebration. Phil Parkinson said: "To beat Arsenal in front of a packed house – it doesn't get much better than that. I am so pleased for the people of Bradford. We want to put Bradford back on the map and I think we are starting to do that." Once the celebrations had subsided, the next question was who would City play in the two-legged semi-final? Would it be a West Yorkshire derby against Leeds United or the glamour team left in the competition Chelsea?

Well, Chelsea thrashed Leeds 5-1 at Elland Road the following week and they were drawn to play Swansea while City would play Aston Villa with the first leg at Valley Parade on 8 January. Whatever the result, City were on a winner financially with director of operations David Baldwin saying the cup run had secured the club's long-term future, adding the two televised ties would bring in an extra £1 million in revenue. There was huge anticipation for the visit of Aston Villa, which attracted another bumper crowd to Valley Parade at 22,245. Villa had been struggling in the Premier League and City felt they could take advantage and yet no one could have forecast how well they would play in taking a two-goal advantage to Villa Park for the second leg. Villa seized the early initiative and Matt Duke twice saved from Belgian international striker Christian Benteke, who also failed to hit the target when well placed. City made Villa pay for these misses when Nahki Wells put them in front after 19 minutes, firing into the net after Zavon Hines' shot rebounded into his path. Both sides had chances before City increased their lead in the 77th minute when Rory McArdle scored with a powerful header from Gary Jones's cross and they almost scored a third when James Hanson's header rebounded off the crossbar. Andreas Weimann temporarily silenced the home crowd when he pulled a goal back for Villa in the 82nd minute only for Carl McHugh to send the City crowd ecstatic again with City's third goal two minutes from the end to leave them dreaming of Wembley.

So, some 6,000 City fans headed to the Midlands on a freezing cold night with snow around hoping that the team could hold on to their two goal advantage, but it was still a huge task against a Premier League side playing at home in front of 40,193. Villa dominated the first half and went in front when Benteke fired home a cross at the far post. City went in at half-time relived to be only one goal down, but they restored their two-goal aggregate lead ten minutes after half-time when James Hanson headed home from Gary Jones's cross in front of jubilant City supporters. Garry Thompson almost scored a second goal only to see his shot rebound from the crossbar and, although Weimann scored a second goal two minutes from the end, it was too late to stop City claiming a third Premier League scalp with their 4-3 aggregate win and booking their place in the Wembley final. The following day they learned that their opponents would be Swansea, who somewhat surprisingly beat Chelsea over two legs.

WEMBLEY HERE WE COME

What an enormous occasion the final turned out to be for Bradford City. Unprecedented media coverage before the game meant that little-known lower division players quickly became household names – like James Hanson, who worked at the local Co-op before City plucked him from non-league Guiseley for £7,500, goalkeeper Matt Duke, who had beaten testicular cancer, Bermudian international Nahki Wells and Garry Thompson, who was planning his fourth appearance at Wembley having played at the national stadium for Morecambe and Scunthorpe. And, they were blessed by their biggest celebrity fan, the Dalai Lama, who was pictured holding the No 14 shirt.

Not since City won the FA Cup in 1911 had one match created so much excitement in the Bradford area and with modern means of communication the Bantams' fame spread throughout the world. The club quickly sold more than 30,000 tickets and some people who had never even seen the team play decided they couldn't miss this eagerly awaited match. It was an emotional day for Bradford fans, who had endured so many disappointing times down the years. Nearly everyone seemed to be waving flags as the teams emerged into the national stadium and there was a special flag to remember the 56 people who died in the Valley Parade fire. Unfortunately, while it proved to be a great occasion, the match was disappointing for City fans as the Bantams were outplayed by their classy Premier opponents and went down 5-0. Although City defended well in the early stages, Swansea penned them back in their own half and it was no surprise when they went in front after 17 minutes, but the two killer goals came either side of half-time. City hoped to hold out until the interval, but conceded a second goal five minutes before half-time and a third two minutes after the break to put the result beyond doubt. More misfortune followed when keeper Matt Duke was sent off for a foul and Swansea scored from the subsequent penalty.

The Swans then rubbed salt into the wounds by scoring a fifth in stoppage time, but the result did not dampen the enthusiasm of the 34,000 City supporters, who defiantly spent the final 20 minutes cheering, singing and waving their flags in a moving and emotional recognition of their club's remarkable journey in reaching a major Wembley final as a League Two side. Not even the 5-0 scoreline could deny that achievement. Parkinson said: "The highlight of the day for me was the way the supporters stayed behind the team throughout the game. I think everybody realised what an enormous achievement this has been from a club from the fourth tier of English football to get to a major final. Of course, I would have loved to be sat here talking about a great performance and a great game, but what Swansea did to us today they have done to Premier League teams. Swansea are a very, very good team. Obviously for our supporters and everybody we would have loved to have made more of a game of it, but it was a tough afternoon."

ROLLER COASTER RIDE TO LEAGUE ONE

No one but no one could have predicted that Bradford City would reach a major cup final at Wembley in 2012-13, but most supporters expected them to be serious candidates for promotion, and if not automatically, then a play-off place was surely a realistic expectation. This feeling tuned in with the board of directors and Phil Parkinson, who recruited extensively during the close season, bringing some experienced players who had enjoyed experience at a higher level than League Two. Among the newcomers was midfield player Gary Jones from Rochdale, whom Stuart McCall had tried to sign, winger or striker Garry Thompson from Scunthorpe, Northern Ireland international defender Rory McArdle from Aberdeen, striker Alan Connell, who had played his part in Swindon's promotion the previous season, left-back James Meredith, a double Wembley winner with York the season before and young players, right-back Stephen Darby from Liverpool, former West Ham youth winger Zavon Hines and young Irish defender Carl McHugh from Reading. To this group was added former loanee, midfield player Nathan Doyle and defender Andrew Davies and midfield player Will Atkinson, who made their loan spells from the previous season permanent by signing contracts.

City achieved their promotion objective but not before taking their supporters on a roller coaster ride interspersed with some extraordinary cup exploits and some frustrating other moments. They gave notice of their promotion credentials by winning five of their first eight matches, but there followed a disappointing spell of four matches without a win – it would be that sort of league season. Despite a mixed set of results as autumn moved into winter – wins against Cheltenham, Northampton, Plymouth, Torquay and Accrington Stanley at home, frustrating defeats against Exeter and Rochdale at Valley Parade – City were still in sixth position on 31 December. There was evidence that City's League Cup exploits affected their league form. Between their thrilling home win over Arsenal on 11 December and their first-leg semi-final victory over Aston Villa on 8 January City won only one of their five league matches. The lead-up to the final after completing their magnificent 4-3 win over

Villa in the two-legged semi-final was not impressive either – one win only in four matches. Yet, the way the team recovered from their drubbing in the Wembley final to win promotion through the play-offs speaks wonders for their character.

City resumed their league campaign 11 points behind seventh placed Cheltenham albeit with matches in hand. Promotion was going to be a tall order, but, after losing only two of their last 15 matches, they finished the regular season in seventh place ready for the play-off campaign. Not surprisingly, City found it difficult to pick up the threads of the league programme after Wembley with scoring goals a particular problem. City went into the match against play-off rivals Exeter City having won one and drawn four matches since the cup final, but, after their 4-1 defeat, their promotion prospects, if not over, at least seemed to be fading. However, City rallied and went on an unbeaten run of six matches (four wins and two draws) producing 14 points and, although promotion rivals Rotherham then beat them 2-0 at Valley Parade ten days before the end of the regular season, the Bantams made sure of their play-off place with a 1-0 win over Burton with one game to spare.

Ironically, City played Burton in the two-legged play off semi-finals and what a shock they gave the Bantams in the first leg at Valley Parade. A crowd of 14,657 gathered, hoping to see City take a giant step towards a second Wembley appearance, but the visitors' striker Calvin Zola silenced the Bantams' supporters by giving Burton a 2-0 lead after six minutes. Nahki Wells pulled a goal back from the penalty spot in the 39th minute before Robbie Weir restored Burton's two-goal advantage just before half-time. City's first-half performance was a huge let-down for home supporters, but they improved after the interval and Garry Thompson scored a crucial goal after 74 minutes to provide the Bantams with a lifeline going into the second leg four days later – a Sunday high noon showdown. City were restricted to an allocation of 1,700 tickets and these were quickly snapped up with some fans queuing through the night. They were not disappointed for Nahki Wells levelled the aggregate scores after 27 minutes and then created an opening for James Hanson to put City 4-3 ahead five minutes after half-time. Burton equalised from the penalty spot five minutes later, but City were not to be denied and Hanson provided an opening for Wells to score the winner – a 3-1 win on the day, 5-4 on aggregate. Parkinson, who had been critical of his team after the first leg, said: "You can't take away the enormity of the achievement. When it mattered the most we produced and I think that's really important. Today was a massive test and we passed it."

WEMBLEY MARK TWO

And so to Wembley where City's opponents were Northampton, a team they had beaten twice in the league and also knocked out of the FA Cup at the first round stage in a penalty shoot-out after a replay. The build-up to Wembley second time around was more low key than for the League Cup Final and fewer fans – 25,000 – made the trip to London, but the match was more important for the long-term development of the club. The players trained at the FA's St George's Park facility as they had done in preparation for the semi-final second-leg match at Aston Villa – the pitch at St George's Park was the same size as Wembley – and there were no suits this time. The players arrived in track suits and, above all, the preparation was kept as normal as possible. Northampton's Bradford-born manager Aidy Boothroyd thought City would be scarred by their defeat against Swansea, but he grossly underestimated the Bantams, who looked fresh and lively from the start even though this was their 64th game of the season whereas Northampton looked startled at the imposing surroundings and never did themselves justice.

City were in command from the start and the game was as good as over by the time they established a 3-0 lead after 28 minutes. Hanson put them in front with a looping header from Thompson's cross after 15 minutes, McArdle added a second four minutes later with a near-post header from Nathan Doyle's cross and Wells scored goal number three after 28 minutes with a close-range volley. City were content to play out the rest of the game and await the post-match celebrations as Northampton rarely threatened in the final hour. Parkinson said: "I was really pleased and couldn't have asked any more from the lads. To be 3-0 up at half-time was a dream really. I think the experience of coming to Wembley before really helped us. I have said all season that when we are at our best we have the power and pace, but we also have the ability to play and it kind of worked perfectly. The size of the pitch suited the running ability of Hanson and Wells and the slickness suited Jones and Doyle in the middle. I thought we got the balance just right."

After spending six seasons in the bottom division, it was a joyful relief to see City win promotion and thousands thronged the centre of Bradford five days after Wembley as the players enjoyed an open-top bus parade to City Hall for a civic reception. City consolidated their place in League One in 2013-14, finishing in 11th place and Parkinson went into his fourth season at the club having refreshed his squad with new players, including defender Alan Sheehan (Notts County), Gary Liddle (Notts County), Billy Clarke (Crawley) and Bill Knott (Sunderland).

WAYNE JACOBS, LEFT BACK WHO PLAYED IN TWO PROMOTION TEAMS IN AN 11-YEAR CAREER AT THE CLUB MAKING OVER 300 APPEARANCES BEFORE BECOMING ASSISTANT MANAGER

SHOOT-OUT SPECIALISTS

No wonder Bradford City have a reputation for penalty shoot-outs. When they knocked Arsenal out of the League Cup at Valley Parade in December 2012 after beating them 3-2 on penalties, it was their ninth successful penalty shoot-out in a row – and four of them came in the memorable 2012-13 season. The first six were in the Johnstone's Paint Trophy. The remarkable sequence began on 6 October 6 2009 when they beat Notts County at home in the JPT and they repeated the feat at home to Port Vale five weeks later in the same competition. City repeated the feat three times in the same competition, all in season 2011-12, beating Sheffield Wednesday at home, and Huddersfield Town and Sheffield United away.

HOT-SHOT WELLS

Bermudian international Nahki Wells was undoubtedly one of the star performers of Bradford City's memorable 2012-13 season, scoring 26 goals in 39 league and cup appearances. He helped them to reach the League Cup Final against Swansea and scored one of the goals in Bradford's second Wembley appearance, the League Two play-off final win against Northampton. He also carried that goalscoring form into the following season after City's promotion to League One, scoring the second hat-trick of his league career in a televised home match against Coventry, the third goal being a stoppage-time equaliser from the penalty spot to earn Bradford a 3-3 draw. However, he made no secret of his desire to play a higher standard of football and in January 2014, he joined West Yorkshire Championship neighbours Huddersfield Town for a reported £1.2 million fee and he made an immediate impact by scoring on his debut. Wells, who once had trials with Dutch club Ajax, played for Dandy Town Hornets and Bermuda Hogges in his home-land before deciding to come to England to attend the Richmond International Academic and Soccer Academy in Leeds and also played with the Bradford non-league club Eccleshill United before breaking into league football with Carlisle United, where former City player Greg Abbott was manager. He made only three appearances with Carlisle in the second half of the 2010-11 campaign before being released and Peter Jackson signed him for City during his brief spell in charge at Valley Parade. Wells was an instant success with the Bantams, scoring 12 league and cup goals in his first season, including a hat-trick in a 3-1 win at Northampton in April 2012. Former City favourite Mark Ellis had links with the soccer academy and Eccleshill and Ellis played a key role in recommending Wells to his old club.

MAGIC JONES

'He's magic, you know, you'll never get past Gary Jones.' That message rang out from Bradford City fans wherever the Bantams captain played and no wonder. For it is difficult to think of a better or more influential signing the club have made in recent years. City had tried to sign Jones before, but finally got their man in the 2012 close season when he was aged 35, having made a record number of 477 appearances for Rochdale, scoring 74 goals. A natural leader, Jones was appointed captain and proved to be an inspiring presence, leading by example with hard work, a will to win, a hatred of losing and no little skill. Not surprisingly, he was voted player of the year in that exceptional first season at Valley Parade. Jones continued to be an influential figure the following season in League One, but, in May 2014, the club decided not to renew his contract and, at 37, he joined Notts County two days before the start of the 2014-15 campaign. Jones began his league career with Swansea in 1997, but during the second half of his first season with the Swans he was loaned to Rochdale, signing permanently at the end of that season. He made 138 appearances during his first spell with Rochdale, scoring 22 goals before being transferred to Barnsley, teaming up with former Rochdale manager Steve Parkin, now assistant at Valley Parade. Jones spent three years at Barnsley, making 56 appearances before re-joining Rochdale, first on loan and then on a permanent basis, becoming club captain. His commitment and determined style of play has endeared him to the fans of the clubs he has played for. He played a key role in Rochdale gaining promotion to League One in 2009-10 and was top scorer the following season – Rochdale's first in the third tier of English football for 36 years.

FIRST INTERNATIONAL

Many players joined City after their international days were over, but in the early years of the club when City were a force in the country, the club boasted several current internationals. City's first international was Jimmy Roberts – all his three Wales caps were gained against Ireland, which was one country in those days, no north and south until 1924. Roberts gained his first cap in 1906 and his other two caps the following year. A full back, Roberts joined City from Crewe in May 1904 and made 24 League and cup appearances over three years before joining Huddersfield Town in June 1909.

The most famous international to wear the City's claret and amber colours was Dickie Bond. Bond's international career was thought to be over when he joined City from Preston in 1909, but he played in all three home internationals – against Ireland, Wales and Scotland in 1910-11 season.

Other England internationals to represent their country while still with City were Evelyn Lintott, who played against Ireland, Scotland and Hungary (twice) in 1909 and outside left Jimmy Conlin, who played against Scotland in 1906. Lintott was signed from Queens Park Rangers in November 1908 – City first season in the First Division – and made

57 League cup appearances over four years before joining Leeds City in 1912. Sadly, he was killed on the Somme in July 1916 while serving with the 1st Yorkshire Regiment. Conlin, the first City player to gain representative honours while playing for the club, when he played for the Football League side, was also killed in action during World War I. He joined City from Albion Rovers a month into the 1904-05 season, scored ten goals in 67 League and cup appearances over two seasons before being transferred to Manchester City in July 1906.

SCOTLAND MAKE JOCK WAIT

The only Scotland international to represent his country while he was on City's books was that great character, goalkeeper Jock Ewart. Ewart was on the verge of the Scotland side when he joined City from Airdrieonians in May 1912 in a £1,200 deal to replace FA Cup final hero Mark Mellors, but he had to wait until 1921 to gain his only international cap – against England. Ewart, who was shell shocked in World War I, played 302 League and cup appearances in two spells at Valley Parade spread over eight peacetime seasons.

City boasts eight Irish internationals – Louis Bookman (one cap), Bobby Campbell (two caps), Harry Hampton (nine caps), Daniel McKinney (one cap), John Murphy (one cap), Sam Russell (two caps) and Frank Thompson (seven caps) and defender Rory McArdle, a hero of the 2012-13 season, who is a regular member of the Northern Ireland squad. Outside left Thompson was a member of City's cup winning team and made 60 League and cup appearances for the Bantams over three seasons after joining them from Irish League side Linfield in 1910 before leaving for Scottish League side Clyde in May 1913.

Right back Sam Russell made 145 league and cup appearances in a five-year spell joined City from Dublin Shelbourne in 1926. After experiencing the heartache of being in the side that were relegated from the Second Division at the end of his first season at Valley Parade in 1926-7, he was an ever present in the team that won the Third Division championship two years later. He left City in 1931 to return to Ireland in 1931 to join Derry City.

JAMAICAN CONNECTION

In recent years, City have had three Jamaican internationals in their team at various times – goalkeeper Donovan Ricketts, winger or striker Jermaine Johnson and winger Omar Daley all signed by Colin Todd. Ricketts, who won more than 60 caps, took over from Australian Paul Henderson when he moved to Leicester City, but lost his place when he was refused re-entry to England after playing in an international because of a work permit problem and joined Village United. Jermaine Johnson, who has played more than 70 times for his country, made an explosive entry into the Bradford City scene in the first half of the 2006-07 season. His electrifying pace frightened League One defences, but City decided to cash in on him and sold him to his present club, Sheffield Wednesday, for a reported £400,000. He has made more than 200 appearances for Wednesday and is the club's longest-serving player. Pacey winger Omar Daley, who has also won more than 70 caps for Jamaica, played 112 matches for City, scoring 14 goals, but his Valley Parade career was badly affected by injury and he struggled for consistency. He was released at the end of the 2010-11 season and joined his former Valley Parade manager Stuart McCall at Scottish Premier League club Motherwell, where he made 39 appearances before he was released in 2013 and joined the North American Soccer League club Minnesota United.

Stuart McCall had a difficult decision to make in 1986 when he was selected for the England and Scotland under-21s teams on the same day. He was qualified to play for both countries because, although he was in Leeds he also qualified for Scotland through his Scottish born father Andy, who played for Blackpool, West Brom, Leeds United and Halifax Town. McCall had been a substitute for England under-21s, but never got on to the field so he was still able to play for Scotland if he chose to do so. He chose Scotland and that proved to be a wise decision for he went on to gain 40 caps for their senior side as well as two under-21 caps.

Defender Andy O'Brien also had to decide where his international future lay. Born in Harrogate, O'Brien was qualified to play for England, but he was also qualified for the Republic of Ireland through his grandfather. He played for England youth and under-21s before switching to Ireland where he also played for their under-21s and has more than 20 appearances for the senior side. O'Brien began his career with City, making 133 League appearances before moving to Newcastle, Portsmouth and Bolton.

Trevor Hockey didn't win international honours with City, but the Keighley born winger or midfield player, who began and finished his career at Valley Parade, won nine caps with his adopted country Wales for which he qualified through family connections. Hockey made his debut at Shrewsbury on 2nd April 1960 as an outside left aged 16 and after making 53 League appearances he joined Nottingham Forest in a £20,000 and went on to play for Newcastle United, Birmingham City, Sheffield United, Norwich City and Aston Villa before returning to City for the 1974-5 season, but he played one more season before he was released. Hockey, who began as a winger before becoming a tough tackling midfield player and, with his long hair, one of the game's great characters, made 523 League appearances in a 16-year career, 97 of them in two spells with City. He sadly died in 1987, aged 43.

WORLD CUP BANTAMS

Former City goalkeeper Mark Schwarzer has played for Australia in two successive World Cup finals tournaments as the Socceroos have gradually emerged as a stronger force in world football. He played for them in the finals in Germany in 2006 while he was a Middlesbrough player and went to the South Africa finals in 2010 after he joined Fulham. He left Fulham in 2013 to join Chelsea as No 2 keeper to Petr Cech.

Another former City goalkeeper, who went to South Africa for the World Cup finals was New Zealander Mark Paston, who played for the Bantams in the old Second Division during the 2003-04 season, making 13 League appearances, but his spell at Valley Parade was blighted by a serious hernia injury, which ruled him out of action for seven months.

He was signed by Nicky Law, but when he returned to the side after his long spell out of action law had been replaced by Bryan Robson and City were involved in their second administration in two years. Paston later played for Walsall before returning to New Zealand, where he now plays for Wellington Phoenix, the only Kiwi team to play in the Australian Hyundai A League. Paston played a crucial role in New Zealand qualifying for the finals. He spent the 2009 Confederation Cup as substitute, but, when first choice Glen Moss was banned for four matches for swearing at the referee in a qualifying match against Fiji, Paston seized his chance, making a vital save from the penalty spot in a qualifying play-off against Bahrain in Wellington. A goal would have sent Bahrain through, but Paston saved the spot kick to guarantee New Zealand a place in the World Cup finals for only the second time in their history. The previous occasion the Rugby Union loving country were in the finals was in Spain in 1982. Paston was first choice as New Zealand were unbeaten in their three group matches, but failed to reach the last 16.

Former City loan player, Aston Villa's Stephen Warnock was part of the England squad for South Africa. Warnock, who spent two months on loan at Valley Parade from Liverpool in the 2002-03 season, making 12 League appearances as a central midfield player and scoring one goal, went to South Africa as understudy to Chelsea left back Ashley Cole. Unfortunately, he did not appear in any of England's four matches as they reached the last 16 of the competition, but went out after a 4-1 defeat against Germany.

CITY IN EUROPE

City made their first European trip in 1908. They received an invitation to play challenge matches in Belgium and Germany after winning the Second Division championship in 1908, The short continental tour

included matches at Verviers and Aix-la-Chappelle, but they had a little problem at the Belgian customs office concerning shin pads. Trainer Charlie Harper brought a full set of shin pads among the luggage, but custom officials did not understand their purpose.

Other officials were called upon to inspect the 'offending luggage' and the pads were slit open because they were suspected of containing contraband. Luckily one of the City party spoke the language and he explained the purpose of the shin pads and they were allowed into the country.

Following their FA Cup triumph in 1911, City received an invitation to play three matches in Scandinavia. They beat Gothenburg Academicals 4-2, which featured a hat-trick from City's England international Dickie Bond, drew 2-2 against a combined Copenhagen side and lost 1-0 against a united Swedish team. Recalling that tour in a newspaper article nearly 40 years, Bond wrote: "The Danes treated us as if we had been Royalty and I remember that I often felt quite embarrassed by some of the attentions they reserved to me. Some of the things their papers said about us were nearly enough to turn our heads if we had been built that way. I will always remember our first game in Copenhagen, not because I was lucky enough to get all three goals, but because I scored one of them with my head. I couldn't help being struck by what a funny game football can be when I thought that I'd been playing in League football back home for eight years and never scored with a header, but then I'd done it abroad straightaway."

City embarked on their most ambitious continental tour in the summer of 1914, playing ten matches in Belgium, Switzerland and Germany within months of the outbreak of World War I. Matches were played at Verviers, Frankfurt, Stuttgart, Mannheim, Pforzheim, Strasburg, Basle, Munich, Zurich and Geneva. Their only defeat was 3-1 against Frankfurt, but the main talking point concerned the airship the Germans flew over the ground during the match. The match was played near an aerodrome that housed a Zeppelin and the airship proved to be a distraction for the City players, who had never seen a Zeppelin before. Bond, who recalls that on the German leg of their tour the players decided to grow military moustaches of the sort the Jerries dearly loved,' complained that 'the incompetence of some of the referees made some of our matches a farce and nearly led to serious trouble.

The Germans had a vastly different idea from ours as to what a foul was and they were allowed to get away with anything short of murder. Their players weren't classy, but the way they set out to stop us from playing our real game would have made all-in wrestlers jealous. After one game at Stuttgart everyone of us was black and blue and I never knew anything like it even in the toughest match in which I ever played in England." He observed: "I never dreamt I would be going back to Germany in khaki uniform and spend three years in a prisoner of war camp in that country."

INTERTOTO ADVENTURE

The only time City have been involved in European competition was in the summer of 2000 after their first season in the Premier League. The idea was the brainchild of chairman Geoffrey Richmond and their European journeys took them to Lithuania to play FC Atlantas in the coastal town of Klaipeda, to Holland to play RKC Walwyck and to St Petersburg where they played FC Zenit – all matches settled over two legs. The first match – in Lithuania – took place a fortnight after Paul Jewell resigned as manager and his deputy, Chris Hutchings, who was appointed the new manager, took charge of the squad for their first taste of European competition. However, there was a hitch before the party left England for, on arrival at Leeds-Bradford Airport on the Saturday morning, they discovered that the aeroplane the club had chartered had developed engine trouble and was unable to fly from Stanstead Airport. Another aircraft was provided for the players while supporters and journalists were provided with a luxury plane on which the Aga Khan travelled regularly for the three hour journey to Klaipeda where it landed at military airport. An under strength City side won the match the following afternoon 3-1 with goals from Isaiah Rankin, Dean Windass and Robbie Blake from the penalty spot. Lee Mills scored twice, Blake and substitute Gareth Grant once as City won the second leg 4-1 in front of a 10,012 crowd at Valley Parade to go through 7-2 on aggregate.

Windass scored twice – one of them a penalty – as City beat RKC Walwyck 2-0 in the first leg at Valley Parade. Mills scored the only goal of the match as City beat them 1-0 in the second leg in Holland the following week and reached the semi-finals after a 3-0 aggregate win. The Bantams met their match against FC Zenit in St Petersburg where they lost the first leg 1-0 before being beaten 3-0 in the second leg at Valley Parade. So, City missed out on the final against Spain's Celta Vigo, who beat Aston Villa in the other 'semi.'

RAVAGED BY WAR

Millions were killed in the carnage of World War I and Bradford City suffered as well as the rest of the community. FA Cup final hero Bob Torrance was killed in action along with reserve players George Draycott, Ernest Goodwin and Harry Potter. Some former players were also killed, among them the FA Cup winning captain Jimmy Speirs along with Evelyn Lintott, James Comrie and Jimmy Conlin. First team Goalkeeper Jock Ewart was wounded and Dickie Bond was taken prisoner. Glasgow born Speirs scored the only of the FA Cup final replay against Newcastle United at Old Trafford in April 1911. He left Valley Parade in December 1912 for a then large fee of £900 to join Leeds City. Speirs, who played for Glasgow Rangers and Clyde before joining City in September 1909, scored 33 goals in 96 League and Cup appearances in three years with the club. He joined the Cameron Highlanders at the outbreak of the war, attained the rank of sergeant and won the Military Medal. He was killed during the Battle of Passchendaele in 1917.

Centre half Torrance replaced William Gildea at the heart of the City defence for the FA Cup final replay to cope with the highly rated Newcastle attack and was widely regarded as man of the match. The auburn haired Scotsman joined City as a right back from his home-town club, Kirkintilloch Rob Roy in 1908 at the age of 20 and was known as the Red Knight of Kirkintilloch. He made 179 League and FA Cup appearances for City and 52 wartime appearances for the club as well as two Scotland trial games. A gunner with the Royal Field Artillery, he was killed in action near Ypres in Belgium and has no known grave.

No current City players died in the Second World War, but former player, inside forward Ernie Tuckett, then with Fulham, was killed in action, as were wartime guest players, Sidney Pugh and Alfred Keeling. Tom Barkas, younger brother of former City favourite Sam Barkas, who had left City to play for Halifax Town, was awarded the British Empire Medal – BEM – for gallantry during the siege of Malta.

'HOPELESSLY INSOLVENT'

The history of Bradford City has been punctuated by financial crises of varying degrees of severity. The club came close to liquidation in the summer of 1928 when the they were described as being in a 'hopelessly insolvent position,' players had received their wages for the last week of the season, the bank were no loner able to provide any further money in view of the club's already large overdraft and no new players had been recruited for the new campaign. Fortunately, supporters' organisations and directors, notably Tom Paton with a donation of £1,250 provided money for the club to continue and the subsequent reconstruction included an inspired move to bring Peter O'Rourke back as manager. The changes brought about immediate success as the following season City won the Third Division North championship and promotion to the Second Division.

As the 1982-3 season drew to a close there were signs that all was not well with the finances with rivals groups bidding to strengthen chairman Bob Martin's board with extra investment or takeover the club. None materialised and on the last Friday in June there was news that the club had decided to oppose a winding up order for an unpaid VAT bill of £17,000 issued by the Inland Revenue.

The petition was due to be heard in the High Court. In the same week, Leeds United issued a winding up order for the £10,000 they owed for player manager Trevor Cherry, signed seven months earlier while it became known that pay cheques of the players had bounced. Then came the news that Bradford Council had appointed Bradford accountant Peter Flesher receiver and the club would be sold to the highest bidder. The total debts of the club amounted to £420,000, of which £250,000 was for unpaid tax bills. The assets totalled only £70,000. Despite the club's desperate financial position, it became known that the directors had turned down a bid of £100,000 for striker Bobby Campbell in the week they went into receivership. After the was appointed, there followed some two months of anxiety for City supporters with various groups bidding for control of the club before Stafford Heginbotham and Jack Tordoff, who had made rival bids, came together to take control with Heginbotham chairman and Tordoff his deputy of a new company, Bradford City (1983) Ltd, the old 1908 company have been wound up when all the debts had been transferred to it. Peter Flescher also joined the board once his duties as receiver were completed. The reformed club had a share capital of £174,262 with Stafford Heginbotham and Jack Tordoff sharing £150,000 equally. Supporters, who were offered shares in £1,000, £500 and £250 units, made the remainder of the share capital.

FIRST ADMINISTRATION

The club was placed in administration twice in three years in 2002 and 2004. They first went into administration on Friday, May 17 2002, triggered by an unpaid Inland Revenue bill of £400,000. There followed an anxious summer for City supporters until the immediate future of the club was secured two days before their first match of the 2002-03 season – a Sky televised match against Wolves at Valley Parade. The re-structuring of the club meant that Geoffrey Richmond, who had been chairman for eight years, left the club and Gordon Gibb, owner of Flamingo Lane theme park in North Yorkshire was appointed chairman with Julian Rhodes, the chief executive.

City went into administration against on Friday, February 27 2004 after it was revealed that the club had defaulted on payments that were due to creditors under the Company Voluntary Arrangement that enabled the club to come out of administration two years previously. That forced City to go back to the High Court again to seek protection from their creditors. It was revealed that the Rhodes family had injected more than £1 million since the previous November to keep the club afloat. City were forced to sell key players like goalscoring striker Andy Gray and full back Simon Francis to Sheffield United while Welsh international midfield player Paul Evans went to Nottingham Forest following a loan spell at Blackpool. City were relegated at the end of the season, manager Bryan Robson made it clear he was no longer interested in continuing as manager and there were serious doubts about the club's future. Supporters rallied round magnificently and raised £250,000 to help the club's survival, including £100,000 at a special fund raising match at Valley Parade, in which several ex-players turned out in a front of a 10,000 crowd.

REPRESENTATIVE MATCHES AT VALLEY PARADE

So keen were the Football League to promote soccer in West Yorkshire in general and Bradford in particular that they staged a representative match less two months after City played their first League match. Despite the inadequate facilities at Valley Parade, not least lack of cover, the ground staged an English League v Irish League match on 10th October 1903. An estimated 20,000 spectators paying £518 crowded into the makeshift ground to see the English League beat the Irish League 2-1.

City also staged an England under-21s match under-21 match against Italy in April 2002 as the FA took international fixtures out into the province and dare, we say, less fashionable venues. The match was well promoted by the FA and the club and Bradford football fans responded by turning up in big numbers, a crowd of 21,642 saw a 1-1 draw.

LIFE OUTSIDE FOOTBALL

Abe Rosenthal was a roly poly character with a smile on his face, who played football for fun – literally. The Liverpool born inside forward, who, unusually, had three separate spells at Bradford City and Tranmere Rovers during his career, once revealed that nearly all his part-time wages of £9 he earned at Tranmere went in tax because his lollipop business was so successful. The revelation came after Rosenthal, who weighed 14 stone, scored the winning goal for Tranmere in an FA Cup third round at Huddersfield Town in January 1952. As the second biggest lollipop manufacturer in the country, he employed more people than the football club that paid his wages. At that time Rosenthal had business interests in Bradford and Manchester – Roscana Lollipops – and employed 25 people in the winter and 50 in the summer. He said: "I just play for the fun of the game now, but I meant to make it my career when I signed for Tranmere in 1938 as a boy of 17.

Goalkeeper Pat Liney, who played for both City and Park Avenue wasn't content to entertain the crowds purely as a football. For, in the evenings he was a popular cabaret singer at night clubs. Liney arrived in Bradford from his native Scotland where he played for his home town club St Mirren in 1966, but he couldn't command a regular place and joined City the following year and went on to make 147 League appearances in four years for the Bantams.

Harry Walden was a man of many parts. The centre forward, signed from Halifax Town in December 1911, six months after City won the FA Cup, he played for the club for nine years, without being able to command a regular place although his goals per games ratio was good 25 in 57 League and cup appearances. His best season was his first with club – he scored 11 goals in 17 League appearances after joining City midway through the campaign and scored a hat-trick in an FA Cup replay against Queens Park Rangers at Valley Parade, which City won 40. He left City in 1920 to join Arsenal, but there was more to Walden than football.

He was a comedian on stage and the only music hall artist to have been an Olympic gold medallist as a member of the Great Britain football team who beat Denmark 4-2 in the final at Stockholm in 1912. He was the principal comedian in a revue that featured a young Hilda Baker making her debut as a leading lady at the Bradford Alhambra theatre in 1921 and he also took the lead role in the first film about football – *The Winning Goal*.

In the days before many clubs had their own youth academies, players came into the professional game from a variety of occupations. Charlie Storer, a member of City's famous half-back line after World War I, was a miner in the Leicestershire coalfield when City spotted him and, not surprisingly, he had no hesitation in accepting the Bantams' offer of a professional contract. Who wouldn't swap a dangerous, unhealthy job underground for his chance to be a full-time professional athlete? At that time, 1913, Storer was earning £1.50 a week as a miner, but manager Peter O'Rourke offered him £2 a week and £4 if he was in the first team. Storer recalled more than 30 years later: "I jumped at the chance. I thought I was a millionaire when I took that turning point in my career."

Another miner, who became a Valley Parade favourite was centre forward Jack Deakin, who, like Charlie Storer, jumped at the chance to play league football rather stay down the pit. Deakin, who came from Altofts in the South Yorkshire coalfield, made his debut part way through the 1936-7 season – City's back in the Third Division North following their relegation from the old Second Division. He made only four appearances, scoring two goals, but was leading scorer the following season with 20 League goals in 30 appearances, plus six in the FA Cup, including four in the 11-3 demolition of non-League Walker Celtic. He was also leading scorer the following season with 23 goals in 28 League appearances. However, war was declared three matches into the next season and he had to go back down the pit to help the war effort and that was the end of his League football career.

IN THE BOARDROOM

A man, who was City chairman on two separate occasions, was that great character Stafford Heginbotham, head of Tebro Toys. He first rescued the club with his friend George Ide in October 1965 when the club was in a parlous state, but, although he improved the financial position of the club, all he had to show for his efforts on the field was promotion from the Fourth Division in 1969 and he gave way to Bob Martin in 1973 after City had dropped back to Division Four. However, ten years later, he and another former director Jack Tordoff came together to buy the club from receiver Peter Flesher after Bob Martin and his board were forced to put City into receivership with debts of £400,000. Two years later City won promotion to the Second Division as Third Division champions and he then had to lead the club through the trauma of the Valley Parade fire disaster and the re-building of the ground before resigning in December 1987, when his vice chairman Jack Tordoff took over.

Jack Tordoff, head of the large motor group, JCT 600, also had two spells at as a director, one of them as chairman. Jack Tordoff first became a director at Valley Parade in 1975, but resigned in January 1978 in protest at the sacking of manager Bobby Kennedy, a decision that split the board. He returned as vice chairman when he Stafford Heginbotham bought the club from the receiver in 1983 and became chairman following Stafford Heginbotham's resignation in 1987. Jack Tordoff, one of Yorkshire's most successful businessmen, prided himself on financial stability – a rare commodity in English football – but after City won promotion to the old Second Division in 1985 he was disappointed when City missed out on promotion to the top division three years later, losing to Middlesbrough in the play-off semi-finals. He resigned in February 1990, handing over the chairmanship to Bradford travel agent David Simpson, but has continued to be club president and has also been a major sponsor of the club over the years.

One of City's most successful – and controversial – chairmen was Geoffrey Richmond, who took over the club in January 1994 from Bradford travel agent David Simpson.

Richmond, who made his money by selling the Ronson lighter company for £10 million after buying it from the receivers. reportedly invested a

£200,000 loan in the club. By the time he left eight and a half years later after City survived their first administration crisis he had made an estimated £8 million from his involvement with the club. The administration was due to Geoffrey Richmond's spending spree in the 2000 close season, described as 'the summer of madness,' but City supporters will also remember him for masterminding their promotion through the play-offs in 1996 and then promotion to the Premier League three years later.

BANTAMS ON TV

One of Sky TV's most popular characters is Chris Kamara, the City manager, who guided the Bantams to promotion through the play-offs in 1995-96 and gave City fans their only Wembley appearance. The versatile, much travelled Kamara arrived at City in the summer of 1994 as one of new manager Lennie Lawrence's signings. His playing days were coming to an end and, when Lawrence's assistant George Shipley left the club towards the end of Lawrence's first season, he became assistant manager and coach. Then, when City sacked Lawrence in November 1995, Kamara succeeded him. Early results were not promising, but, in the last two months of the season, they improved dramatically and, after losing only three of their last 16 matches, City sneaked into the Third Division play-offs. They beat Blackpool 3-2 on aggregate in the two legged semi-final despite losing the first leg 2-0 at Valley Parade before beating Notts County 2-0 in the final at Wembley in front of a 39,000 crowd, 30,000 of them from Bradford. Kamara made wholesale changes the following season with several foreign players appearing at Valley Parade along with former England international Chris Waddle. City survived by beating Charlton Athletic 3-0 in the last match to ensure survival, but results did not go Kamara's way the following season and, after losing 2-0 at Manchester City in the FA Cup third round on the first Saturday in January chairman Geoffrey Richmond sacked Kamara.

He had a brief and unsuccessful spell as manager at his old club Stoke City before turning his back on football management and embarking on a TV career, where his enthusiastic approach coupled with a sharp, analytical football brain has made him a huge favourite with the viewers. 'It's unbelievable Geoff' is one of his favourite rapport lines with the equally popular and football enthusiast Geoff Stelling. Winger Peter Beagrie was one of City's most popular players from their Premier League era. The former Middlesbrough, Sheffield United, Stoke City, Everton and Sunderland winger arrived at Valley Parade in a £50,000 deal from Manchester City in the 1997 close season after City had survived their first season in the old First Division and helped them to gain promotion to the Premier League two years later. He made 146 league and cup appearances for City, scoring 23 goals before joining Scunthorpe United and helping them to gain promotion from League Two in 2004-5. He later signed for Grimsby Town, but retired one year later to concentrate on a career in television with ITV and Sky. Later he signed a contract with Sky and is involved in coverage of Champions, Leagues One and Two divisions.

Striker Don Goodman began his career with City as an 18-year-old apprentice electrician with Leeds City Council in 1984, but could not command a regular first team place. However, his subsequent £50,000 move to West Brom proved to be the springboard for a successful career, which saw him play for Sunderland and Wolves. He wound down his career at Barnsley on loan, Walsall and Exeter and he also had spells with Motherwell and with the Japanese side San Hiroshima while gradually moving into television where he is now seen and heard regularly on Sky TV.

Striker Steve Claridge was nearing the end of his long career when manager Colin Todd signed him in 2005 and he spent a year at Valley Parade, scoring some important goals without being able to establish a regular place in the starting line-up.

As he wound down a playing career spanning more than 20 years, the man whose former clubs included Birmingham City, Leicester City and Portsmouth among others moved into radio and television as a summariser. He worked for Setanta TV before its demise and is now hear regularly on Radio Five as well as the late night Football League Show that the BBC introduced in the 2009-10 season. Former manager Paul Jewell also worked regularly on Sky TV and on BBC Radio Five.

BRADFORD FOOTBALL RIVALRY

Only older supporters remember the fierce rivalry between the two Bradford clubs – City and Park Avenue. The last League match between the clubs took place at Park Avenue on Saturday, January 25 1969. Park Avenue were voted out of the Football League the following year in favour of Cambridge United after their fourth successive re-election application and, since then, there have been only friendly matches between the two clubs. The first time he clubs met was in the first year of Park Avenue's existence. The newly formed club could not gain election to the Second Division of the Football League at first so they joined the Southern League, which shows just determined the founding fathers of Park Avenue were to establish football in their part of the city considering how much travelling was involved and how difficult travel could be in those days. However, as well as playing in the Southern League, Avenue also entered a side in the North Eastern League and it was at that level that the two Bradford clubs met on a Tuesday afternoon, November 19, 1907. Although it could only be regarded as a reserve team match, a remarkably

large crowd of 14,000 turned out to see City win 2-1 with goals from Frank O'Rourke and George Handley

City also beat Avenue 2-1 in the West Yorkshire Cup final at Park Avenue in April 1908 with goals both goals being scored by Frank O'Rourke. The match took place three days after the Bantams' Second Division championship season ended with a 2-0 home win over Lincoln City.

Avenue gained election to the Second Division in the summer of 1908 as City moved into the First Division and the clubs actually met in the FA Cup two years before their first League meeting – February 24 1912. A goal from Frank O'Rourke settled that third round tie in front of a 24,833 crowd. It was the first of three FA Cup ties between the clubs. The second was a second round tie Park Avenue on December 15 1951 when both clubs were in Division Three North. Park Avenue beat City that day 3-2 in front of a 24,430 crowd. The teams also met in a second round tie at Park Avenue on December 6 1958 when City won 2-0 with John McCole scoring both goals. The crowd that day was 19,962. The first League match between City and Avenue was a First Division fixture at Valley Parade on October 24 1914, nearly three months after World War I had started and many in the 29,802 crowd wore army uniforms. They saw City win 3-2 with from goals from Charlie Storer, Oscar Fox and Jimmy McIlvenny. Avenue gained their revenge with a 3-0 win in the return match in the last match of the season before League football was suspended for four seasons because of the war.

RELEGATION AT THE DOUBLE

The two Bradford clubs played each other in wartime football and when the League programme resumed in 1919-20, both matches ended in 0-0 draws. The following season was the last in which City and Avenue would each other in top-flight football. City won both matches 2-1 that season, but Avenue were relegated at the end of the campaign and the following season both clubs went down. City were relegated from Division One while Avenue became the first club to suffer the indignity of relegation for the second season in a row, going down to Third Division North, which had been formed the year before.

Meetings between the two Bradford clubs resumed in Division Three North in 1927-8 after City were relegated from the Second Division and City lost both of them – 3-2 at Valley Parade before a massive 37,059 crowd – a record for a Bradford derby – with the Bantams being guilty of missing two penalties and 5-0 at Park Avenue.

Park Avenue went back to the Second Division as Third Division North champions that season with City finishing in sixth place. However meetings between the wool city rivals resumed after a season's break when City joined Avenue in the Second Division after they too won the Third Division North championship in 1928-9.

The clubs have met only one in the League Cup, a remarkable first round tie at Park Avenue in September 1963, when Avenue beat City 7-3. Rodney Green with two goals and John Hall were City's scorers. The crowd was 6,593. That defeat was part of a bad start to the season that saw City fail to won any one of their opening five League matches – four defeats and a draw adding to a miserable start to the campaign.

Several players have played for both clubs, but the only exchange deal between the clubs took place in February 1938 when Jimmy Robertson moved from Avenue to City and Jack Gallon moved in the opposite direction.

BOBBY STARS FOR BOTH CLUBS

Bradford born striker Bobby Ham enjoyed two spells at both clubs, making 159 League appearances and scoring 53 goals for Park Avenue and 187 League appearances and 64 goals for City. When he signed for City the first time he scored a goal that helped Avenue to beat the Bantams 2-1 at Valley Parade on February 10 1968 and then played for City in their 1-1 at Crewe the following Saturday after his £2,500 transfer.

Another player, who played for both clubs was Bradford born half back Donald Duckett, who joined City as a 20-year-old from a junior club at Queensbury in April 1914, four months before the outbreak of World War I. Although the war delayed his start in League football, he established himself in wartime football and topped City's wartime appearance, playing in 123 matches in four seasons, scoring 20 goals. So, by the time the League programme resumed after the war, he was a regular in the team and quickly became part of the famous Hargreaves-Storer-Duckett half back line.

Duckett, whose wage in 1919 was £6 a week during the football season, was City's regular left half in their last three seasons in the First Division and was an ever present with 42 appearances in their relegation season. He continued to play for the club in the Second Division, but he made only three appearances in what turned out to be his last season at Valley Parade and was transferred to Halifax Town in December after making 165 League and cup appearances spread over ten seasons plus his wartime matches. He spent almost three seasons playing for Halifax in the Third Division North before he joined Park Avenue. He helped them win promotion back to the Second Division from Third Division North and was made captain after they were promoted before being forced to retire with knee trouble in March 1929.

The eight players who have played for both clubs in derby matches are Jimmy Anders, Charlie Atkinson, Dick Conroy, Bobby Ham, Arnold Kendall, Gerry Lightowler, Pat Liney, Polly Ward. The first of these players to play against both clubs was centre half Dick Conroy, who turned out for Park Avenue against City in December 1953 having played for City against Park Avenue six times in Bradford derby matches.

Right winger Jack Padgett made only three League appearances in his brief career, but, remarkably, he played for both Bradford clubs, scoring a goal for each club – for City in 1937-8 and for Park Avenue the following season.

TOP DERBY CROWD

The highest crowd for a Bradford derby match was at Valley Parade on Saturday, September 17 1927, when Park Avenue beat City 3-2 in front of 37.059. It was the first derby match for seven years. The previous time they met both clubs were in the First Division. Since then they had been relegated two divisions to Third Division North.

Two men have managed both City and Park Avenue, Peter O'Rourke, who led to the their FA Cup triumph in 1911 and David Steele, who was in charge for four season just after the Second World War.

It's unlikely to happen nowadays, but two players were married in the morning before appearing in Bradford derby matches in the afternoon. The first time it happened was on November 23 1935 when goalkeeper Chick Farr appeared for Avenue in their Second Division match at home to City in the afternoon after being married in the morning. The result was a 1-1 draw. Also, Roy Ellam played for City in their Fourth Division match against Avenue at Valley Parade on February 22 1964 after he had been married in the morning. City won 1-0.

After Park Avenue were voted out of the League in 1970, they joined the Northern Premier League and played at their own ground for another three years before selling it. That left them without a home of their own and so they arranged to play 'home' matches at Valley Parade. However, it soon became clear that the club were struggling financially as gates struggled to reach 1,000 and they decided to go into voluntary liquidation with debts of £9,000. Their first match was a 2-2 draw against Northwich Victoria on 11th August 1973 with a crowd of 1,022. The last match was played on 2nd May 1974 where a meagre crowd 698 saw Park Avenue a 1-0 win over Great Harwood, Mike Fleming scoring the winner in the last minute.

FIRE DISASTER

The word disaster is glibly used by football fans and sports journalists to describe nothing more serious than a home defeat or injury to a key player. As far as I am concerned and, I am sure I speak for all City followers, there has been only one disaster connected with the Bantams and that was the Valley Parade fire tragedy on Saturday, May 11, 1985 when 56 people lost their lives when fire swept through the main stand. A crowd of more than 11,000 had gathered to watch City's final match of the season against Lincoln City – and to see captain Peter Jackson and the team receive the Third Division championship trophy. The trophy was presented and Jackson led his team-mates on a lap of honour before the match began before triumph turned to tragedy.

The fire started under some bench seating towards the back of the wooden stand just before half-time and the referee took the players off the field. Within minutes, the fire, fanned by the wind, spread rapidly to the roof and quickly engulfed the stand. Fifty six people died and hundreds were badly burned. The fire had a devastating effect not just on the families concerned but on the whole community and memories are still raw to this day. Those who died are remembered at a short service around a memorial made by Bradford's twin town of Hamm on the 11 May every year.

WARTIME FOOTBALL

When World War I broke out in August 1914, the Football League decided to go ahead with their League programme, reflecting the optimistic mood in the country that the war would be over by Christmas. That optimism proved to be tragically mistaken as the war went on for more than four years with tragic loss of life as millions were killed in battle. City finished a respectable tenth in the First Division in the 1914-15 season and reached the fourth round of the FA Cup before losing 2-0 at home to Everton. However, when it became clear that the wear would not be over any time soon, the Football Association bowed to the inevitable and suspended all professional football indefinitely. However, it was considered that football should continue in some form and so there followed four years of wartime football played on a regional basis with clubs able to use guest players from other clubs, who found themselves stationed at nearby garrisons. Some players, including Dickie Bond and Bob Torrance went to the front, with Bond joining the Bradford Pals, part of the 18th Battalion of the West Yorkshire Regiment while other worked in munitions factories. City found themselves in the Midland Section playing Yorkshire clubs and Midland teams like Birmingham, Leicester and the two Nottingham clubs. The competition didn't mean much in football terms, but it was credited with boosting morale and kept the clubs ticking over.

Donald Duckett played most wartime games for City – 123 – over four seasons while Jimmy McIlvenny made 111 appearances and was top scorer with 65 goals. However, with many men away at war attendances dropped to about 1,000 and City's net loss at the end of the war was £6,345 and bank overdraft of £9,338 – large totals in those days.

The football authorities adopted a different policy when World War Two broke out in September 1939, suspending the League programme after just three matches had been played. City had made an inauspicious start with two defeats – at home to Accrington Stanley and away to New Brighton before earning a 2-2 draw at Barrow on Saturday, September 2. The players returned home from Barrow that night and the following – at 11am – war was declared with Germany following their invasion of Poland. City played some friendly fixtures before the wartime regional competitions began on October 21.

SHACK SCORES FIVE

The Bantams took terrible beatings at the hands of their neighbours Bradford Park Avenue during the war. In December 1942, Avenue thrashed them 10-0 and a year later they enjoyed an 8-0 win, with Len Shackleton scoring five and George Ainsley the other three. They also suffered another spectacular defeat in November 1944 when Newcastle United beat them 11-0 at St James' Park with the Magpies' guest player Eddie Carr, who later played for City, scoring six goals. Shackleton had a unique experience on Christmas Day 1940, playing for both Bradford clubs on the same day. He played for his own club Park Avenue at Leeds United in the morning and for City at Huddersfield Town in the afternoon when he scored a rare headed goal in the Bantams' 4-3 win. Shackleton, dubbed the Clown Prince of Soccer because of his practical jokes, was one of the best footballers Bradford has ever produced. He caused controversy and no little amusement when, he included a chapter on what this on what the average football director knows about football. The page was blank! Born in 1922, he was 17 when war was declared and, although he played seven League matches for Park Avenue after the war, he was clearly destined for bigger things and was soon on the move to First Division Newcastle United.

He then moved to North East rivals where he spent the bulk of his career, scoring 97 League goals in 320 matches before retiring in 1957. He died in 2000 and a superb exhibition covering his playing career is on display at the Park Avenue clubhouse at Horsfall Playing Fields in Bradford.

Few good things came out of wartime football for City, but they did unearth an outstanding player in wing half Joe Harvey. Born at Edlington in South

Yorkshire, Harvey was initially signed by Park Avenue as an 18-year-old in 1936, but he did not play in the League for them. He did not play a League match at his next club Wolves and it was only when to his third club Bournemouth that he made his League debut, playing 37 matches for them before moving back to Bradford to play for City in the 1938 close season. Frustratingly for Harvey, manager Fred Westgarth did not play him in the following season – the last before war was declared, but he eventually established himself as a regular in wartime football, making 126 appearances and scored 39 goals. Unfortunately for City supporters, they didn't get the chance to see Harvey play for the club in peacetime because, before the Football League programme in 1946 he got his big move to Newcastle United where he made 224 League appearances, winning an FA Cup winner's medal in 1951 before becoming their manager.

GREAT ESCAPES

What a struggle it was for City to retain their First Division status the following season. Team strengthening was clearly needed and manager Peter O'Rourke made several changes bringing in future England centre half Evelyn Lintott from Queens Park Rangers, winger William Grimes from Glossop North End, centre forward Bob Whittingham from Blackpool, who scored a valuable ten goals in the last 17 matches, England amateur international outside left, Harry Hardman from Manchester United, left back George Chaplin from Dundee and goalkeeper Mark Mellors for £350 from Sheffield United. City ended the season with three home matches, but, after beating Chelsea 3-0 they let slip a 2-0 lead against Notts County and had to settle for a 2-2 draw.

At that stage, it seemed that relegation was inevitable, but relegation rivals Manchester City lost at Bristol City and that gave City the chance of escape of they could beat Manchester United in their last match at Valley Parade the following evening – Thursday 29th April, 1909. Some 30,000, including the Manchester City team were present in a 30,000 crowd to create a tense, highly charged atmosphere. City hopes rose as Frank O'Rourke gave them the lead in the first half, but they had to withstand some determined and, at times frantic pressure, but they managed to hang on to their lead and their 1-0 victory was enough to ensure First Division survival and condemn Manchester City to relegation with Leicester Fosse (now City). Supporters ran on to the pitch to goalkeeper hero Mark Mellors should high from the field. Near the end Mellors had been knocked out as he threw himself in the path of a fierce shot and was propped in goal as City defended the subsequent corner. Recalling the match nearly 40 years later, Mellors, who had joined City only a month beforehand, wrote: "It looked odds on our being relegated to the Second Division. When we met Manchester United, who had just won the FA Cup we had to win to escape.

If United either drew or won it meant safety for their City neighbours, who were two points in front of us. All the city team and their directors came to watch their neighbours make a valiant fight on their behalf and an encounter truly worth describing as hair-raising was witnessed by the excited crowd. The tension was so great that many nervous spectators with weak hearts had to go away because they could not stand the strain. Every kick of the match was watched with rapt attention and the demonstration when Frank O'Rourke gave us the lead in the first half was more than any words of mine cane do justice to. It was all a question of whether we could keep our lead which everybody agreed had been worthily won. Mellors went to quote a team-mate, who described how a shot from a City player had hit the goalkeeper in the stomach and felled him to the ground and how he had been 'propped up between the sticks after a long wait to revive him after the ball had kicked out of play for a corner.

'Everybody held his breath while the ball hovered in the danger zone and when somebody banged it away there was a sigh of relief which could have been heard a mile off.' The unnamed player went to describe 'thousands of watches were held in the hands of anxious spectators' in the last five or ten minutes and after Mellors had been carried shoulder high off the field it was found that his was black and blue where the ball had hit him. Mellors added: "What a scene there was when the referee his whistle for time. The spectators flocked on to the ground and the cheering, long and wild, must have rolled over the city like distant thunder."

General election 1997 has a special place in British political history. The Conservatives, who had been in power with first Margaret Thatcher and then John Major as Prime Minister for 18 years lost in a landslide to the Labour Party headed by Tony Blair. However, as voters were going to the polls that Thursday evening, 1st May, City supporters gathered at Valley Parade knowing that they needed to beat Charlton Athletic in a re-arranged match and then Queens Park Rangers in the last match on the Sunday to be certain of surviving in the First Division following promotion through the play-offs 12 months earlier.

BROTHERS IN ARMS

There have been several instances of brothers appearing for City. The first were the Logan brothers, Scots Jimmy and Peter. Both joined the club from the Scottish junior club Edinburgh St Bernard's. Jimmy made only five appearances in a 17 month spell at Valley Parade before moving to Chesterfield in August 1906. However, Peter, who joined City two years later became one of the great figures in the clubs's history during his 17-year career at Valley Parade, playing in a variety of positions as he scored 43 goals in 304 League and cup matches, including the FA Cup final in 1911.

Winger Peter Middleton joined City from Sheffield Wednesday in May 1968 and played in the Fourth Division side the following season. He was transferred to Plymouth Argyle in September 1972 when City had been relegated after scoring 34 goals in 151 League and cup appearances. He was tragically killed in a road accident in 1977. His younger brother John was a key figure in City's defence in the 1976-7 Fourth Division promotion team and made 214 League and cup appearances in a six year spell.

Peter and David Jackson were the twin sons of manager Peter Jackson, joining the club when their father became manager in March 1955. They played regularly for the first team, inside forward David scoring 68 goals in 275 League and cup appearances while half back Peter played 217 matches, scoring 15 goals. After leaving Valley parade, when their father was sacked they played together for two seasons at Tranmere Rovers.

THE BARKAS SOCCER BOYS

All five Barkas brothers played League football and two of them, Sam and Tom played for City. Left back Sam made 216 League and cup appearances in six years at Valley Parade before leaving in April 1934 for Manchester City and later gained five England caps. Inside forward Tom played for City at the same time as Sam, making 16 appearances before he left in December 1934 to join Halifax Town. He scored 35 goals in 169 League appearances before continuing his career with Rochdale, Stockport and Carlisle. Scottish international winger Arthur Graham signed for City in June 1985, two months after they gained promotion to the old Second Division. Graham, a former Leeds United team-mate of player manager Trevor Cherry joined the club from Manchester United and made 37 League and cup appearances before becoming youth team coach. His younger brother, left back Jimmy played seven games for City in 1988-9 before moving to Rochdale first on loan and then in a permanent transfer. After making 137 League appearances for Rochdale he moved to Hull City.

There were high hopes of Michael Boulding when he joined City in July 2008 along with his brother, fellow striker Rory Boulding. Michael had been top scorer with Mansfield Town when they were relegated to Conference the season and City manager Stuart McCall hoped he achieve a similar goalscoring record at Valley Parade. Unfortunately, it didn't happen like that and Michael was released in March 2010 by new manager Peter Taylor, a month after McCall left the club along with brother Rory. Rory, who made only a handful of first team appearances, joined Accrington Stanley in July 2010 while Michael was having a trial at Barnsley (at the time of writing)

CRICKETERS TURNED FOOTBALLERS

Brian Close prides himself as an all-round sportsman and with justification. A long career as an all-round cricketer and captain with Yorkshire, Somerset and England and a single handicap golfer, Close was no mean footballer in his younger days. A centre forward, Close was on Arsenal's books when he joined City in October 1952 and he scored five goals in nine League and cup appearances before Yorkshire, concerned that he might get injured, persuaded him to concentrate on cricket. Perhaps his best performance was scoring two goals in City's 4-0 home win over non-League Rhyl Athletic in the FA Cup first round in November 1952. He also scored in the 1-1 draw against Ipswich in the next round – City were beaten 5-1 in the replay.

Bradford-born Yorkshire wicketkeeper, David Bairstow was also a bustling centre forward, who made 17 appearances, scoring one goal in the 1971-2 and 1972-3 seasons before he too was persuaded to concentrate solely on cricket. Bairstow, who later captained Yorkshire, sadly died in 1998.

GHOST HUNTING

Infamous New Year celebrations in 1922 have passed down in City's folklore. They involved three Scottish players, one time record signing Billy Watson, goalkeeper Jock Ewart and Tommy Robb. They were charged with being in enclosed premises not far from Valley Parade 'with intent to commit a felony.' Fortunately for the players, the Bradford magistrates believed their explanation hat this was a 'ghost hunting' expedition – a foolish prank that went wrong.

Watson gave the definitive version in a newspaper article more than 20 years later. He said the trouble started when 'three respectable Scottish citizens of Bradford' were arrested by platoon of policemen at the back of a house in Oak Avenue. The house was next to that occupied by the Chief Constable of Bradford at the time, but the players didn't know that and they must have disturbed him as they pushed his bedroom window up and started questioning him. They threw a few harmless, but accurate snowballs and told him to get to bed after wishing him a Happy New Year. Then police up went the window again, the Chief Constable told his officers to arrest the 'desperadoes', who were lodged in jail overnight before being taken to court the following morning and then heard the case dismissed as a 'foolish prank' after paying for damage to a house that had stood neglected for 20 years. Watson said that 'was the first and last mission' of looking for ghosts. It had started through a rumour that the house was haunted. A few months later, the house was occupied so the 'desperadoes' must have done some good, said Watson.